"SAIGON HAS FALLEN."

SAIGON HAS FALLEN

PETER ARNETT

Saigon Has Fallen
Copyright © 2015/2018 by Peter Arnett

ISBN-13: 978-0-9990359-4-8.

Cover design by Brehanna Ramirez
Interior design by Jay McNair

All photos from AP Images,
www.apimages.com, and the Peter Arnett Collection

All archival material courtesy of
Associated Press Corporate Archives, New York, NY

Cover photograph: A U.S. Marine helicopter takes off
from helipad on top of the American Embassy in
Saigon, Vietnam, Apr. 30, 1975 (AP Photo/Phu).

Frontispiece photograph: People try to scale the 14-foot wall
of the U.S. Embassy in Saigon, trying to reach evacuation
helicopters, as the last of the Americans depart from
Vietnam, Apr. 29, 1975. (AP Photo/Neal Ulevich)

Ch. 2 photos: "Saigon AP: A Short Guide to News Coverage
in Viet Nam" by Malcolm Browne, 1963. Malcolm Browne
Papers, Box 3. AP Corporate Archives, New York.

Ch. 10 photos: George Esper, [South Vietnam
Surrender], Apr. 29, 1975. Wirecopy, Various Wires,
Oversize Folder. AP Corporate Archives, New York.

*For my news colleagues during the Vietnam War
who risked death to get the story*

CONTENTS

1

"SAIGON HAS FALLEN."

A RTILLERY EXPLOSIONS sound a fearsome 4 a.m. wake-up call, but I'm already awake. Impatient for victory, the attackers waiting at the gates of a vanquished Saigon have been warning they would act, and now with each thump of the Soviet-made 130 mm guns, their shells landing a mile or so away, sound waves rustle the curtains of my open seventh-floor hotel window. As I reach for my water glass, it trembles, and me with it. The final full day of the Vietnam War is beginning.

Streetlights shine below as I look out toward Tan Son Nhut airport,* once described as the busiest in the world when America was waging war here. Now it is burning from one end to the other, the flames brilliantly lighting up the sky. There will be two more

---

* This and many other Vietnamese place names have an alternate spelling today, but I use the spellings commonly used at the time of the war.

hours of the darkness, but this seems like a new dawn rising, an appropriate description, I think later, of the intentions of those wreaking havoc on the airport. The commanders of North Vietnam's military juggernaut, pressing for victory after a 50-day rout of their South Vietnamese opponents, are pushing open the gates of the capital. They will force a new dawn on South Vietnam, America's once favored ally, as it loses its 20-year struggle to remain an independent, pro-western state. As I write these still vivid memories of the end of the war, and the role that my reporter colleagues and I played in covering it, I find it hard to believe that four decades have passed since April 1975.

After watching the destruction of the airport, I phone the Associated Press office a few blocks away, and my colleague Ed White answers. He and George Esper, the bureau chief, have been up all night working the telex communications link with our New York headquarters. Our editors are anxious for the latest developments in a story that has gripped the world. White tells me the American Embassy confirms major damage at the airport with the runways probably unusable. American planners have been intending to airlift out of the country several thousand more vulnerable Vietnamese allies today, but what can they do now? The popular adage, Murphy's Law, which warns, "Anything that can go wrong will go wrong," will be proven time and time again today, in the final hours of bitter defeat for the losers and a historic victory for the winners.

Knowing this will be a long day, I take my time as I shower and dress, then go upstairs to the hotel dining room, which is serving hot coffee, and walk out to the balcony for a better view. Daylight is approaching, and I can clearly see thick black smoke hanging over the airport like a funeral shroud. I'm joined by a few news colleagues, chatting animatedly, in awe of what is happening, knowing we are watching momentous history unfold right before our eyes.

As the sky brightens, we see a Vietnamese air force transport plane, a De Havilland Caribou, rise sharply into the air high above Tan Son Nhut airport. Suddenly, it seems to break in half, bursting into flames and falling in pieces to the ground. Stricken silent by this horrifying spectacle, we see a second aircraft following the same path soon afterward and suffering the same fate, like the first undoubtedly a victim of ground fire. It seems there'll be no escape for anyone from the airport today.

At the American Embassy, Ambassador Graham Martin is in disbelief, committed as he is to evacuating as many vulnerable Vietnamese as possible before the communists arrive. He insists on personally checking the airport tarmac, alarming those who warn of great risk from approaching enemy. After the war, Martin would tell me, "It didn't make sense to me that we couldn't physically come in with transport planes. I wanted to check it for myself, to make my own judgment. It would have made a difference. We could have gotten five or ten thousand more people out."

Martin has another reason for the airport visit, a token of respect to what he views as hallowed ground. An earlier offer from Washington to send in a small U.S. Marine detachment to secure the airport evacuation area was turned down, and some members of the embassy's own Marine guard are used. In the early morning shelling, two of the Marines are killed, Charles McMahon and Darwin Judge, the last two American servicemen to die in Vietnam. Martin knows them both well. And he thinks of his foster son, First Lieutenant Glenn Dill Mann, killed in action in Vietnam on Dec. 8, 1965, when hit by machine-gun fire while flying his armed helicopter against an enemy position south of Chu Lai.

Reaching the airport, Martin finds a usable runway amidst the still-burning buildings, but little security. He worries about a repeat of the earlier airport panics in Danang and Nhatrang that had hundreds of desperate people fighting with soldiers and police to get on departing rescue aircraft. He tells me, "I decided it was not worth the risk. I picked up the phone and I told Secretary Kissinger to inform the president that we have to go to Option Four immediately, to the helicopter airlift for the remaining Americans, and as many Vietnamese as we can take." But Martin's urgent instruction is lost somewhere down the line. The airlift does not begin for several hours.

Option Four is code for Operation Frequent Wind, planned to be the biggest such evacuation in history, moving people to American Navy ships off the coast. Most of the passengers for the final helicopter lifts have been chosen in advance, alerted to keep listening to Armed Forces Radio. When the time comes to move they will hear the signal, Bing Crosby's song "White Christmas," playing continuously, with an occasional break for the Sousa march "The Stars and Stripes Forever." Thirteen helicopter pickup points have been selected around Saigon, using the small UH-1 Huey ships for the tops of tall buildings and the much bigger CH-53 Sea Knights for the American Defense Department compound at the airport and the embassy grounds.

The essential personnel waiting to depart include the large contingent of international journalists covering the story for the world's media. During the past week some have considered the possibility of remaining behind and seeing what transpires, but their home offices expect them to leave with the last Americans because of the uncertainty of the future. I know that Esper wants to stay. He's been here too long to miss the final moments of his most important story. Me too, and I message AP president Wes Gallagher, explaining that because I was here at the war's beginnings it's worth the risk to document the final hours. Gallagher is less supportive of the presence of Matt Franjola, an AP reporter in the region for several years. Esper sends a message to his boss: "Request you please reconsider..." Gallagher does. The three of us will stay.

As I drive through the city, I see that crowds are gathering at intersections and arguing. Several million people are now estimated to be living in Saigon, many of them recent refugees from the countryside. Not everyone wants to leave, but several hundred thousand believe their lives have been compromised in the eyes of the Communists by their association with America and its policies, and are desperate to get out. I drive by Saigon's port and see small ships crowded with people setting off down the river.

The former CIA analyst Frank Snepp remembered that time in an interview with me after the war: "The city was holding its breath. We had always feared that the Vietnamese would mob us if we ever tried to leave. But they realized on that last day that we were their last hope. If they turned against us, there was no way out of the country."

No one is killed in the shameful melees that are to follow, but the mad scrambles to go anywhere but Vietnam still remain today an ignominious coda to the already bleak history of America's last years in Vietnam. The main crisis unfolds in and around

6

the U.S. Embassy, a distinctive six-story white building with a concrete lattice facade that serves to keep
the building cool and deflect incoming missiles. It is
located on Unification Street, opposite the British
Embassy, next to the French, and two blocks from the
presidential palace.

I'd seen some people hanging around the embassy
earlier in the day, but when the helicopters start
emerging from the leaden afternoon skies to pick
up the chosen few, a stampede begins. By late afternoon an estimated 10,000 desperate Vietnamese have
advanced on the embassy, pushing and shoving to get
close to the iron gates and the high walls, and when
they do get there, endeavoring to claw themselves
over. The U.S. Marine security force strives to get control, only to meet with shouted protests and insults.

That evening, April 29, 1975, I write a story for the
AP that begins, "Ten years ago I watched the first U.S.
Marines arrive to help Vietnam. They were greeted on
the beaches by pretty Vietnamese girls in white silken
robes who draped flower garlands about their necks. A
decade has passed, and on Tuesday I watched the U.S.
Marines shepherding Americans out of South Vietnam. They were the same clean-cut–looking young
men of a decade ago. But the Vietnamese were different. Those who didn't have a place for them on
the last helicopters—and there were thousands left
behind—hooted, booed and scuffled with the Marines

trying to secure the landing zones. Some Vietnamese threw themselves over walls and wire fences, only to be thrown back by Marines. Bloodshed was avoided seemingly only by good luck and bad aim on the part of some angry Vietnamese who shot at a few departing buses and helicopters."

There are also mixed signals and questionable decisions. When the Sea Knight helicopters are being shifted to the embassy for evacuations in late afternoon, Ambassador Martin seems reluctant to allow the felling of his favorite tamarind tree in the parking lot so the big ships can land. Marines chop it down, anyway. As evening arrives, there is a growing awareness that some of the 13 designated pickup points have not been visited by any helicopters, leaving some of the most vulnerable Vietnamese, many of them CIA workers, to the mercy of the arriving communists.

Frank Snepp is inside the embassy that night, and tells me later, "Americans have been criticized that day in Saigon for their sins of omission, but the heroes that day were the embassy officers who pursued their way through the crowds and risked their lives to get their friends on those helicopters. If the Americans salvage anything of their honor from the last day of the war it is due to the young men who did the legwork during the evacuation while the ambassador and his aides sat back in the embassy trying to figure out what went wrong."

The monsoon is coming to Saigon, with heavy downpours of nighttime rain, arriving along with the North Vietnamese, who from the beginning of this offensive have been in a race against the weather. They know the heavy tanks and artillery pieces they use to support their overwhelming conventional attacks can easily bog down in the mud. From the slippery roof of the Eden Building, where the AP office is located, I watch through the rainy mist as the dark shapes of helicopters come and go. In the streetlights below people are staring into the dark sky and at the twinkling navigation lights of the flights to freedom, so near but yet so far. Many of them carry small bags and sacks in their hands, desperate for any ride out.

At 2 the following morning, April 30, the U.S. Embassy needs to destroy all its communications equipment in preparation for final departure. This means messages have to be sent via helicopter to the Navy ships, where they're passed to Washington, and return messages follow the same slow process in reverse.

Martin refuses to leave until all the people he feels responsible for are evacuated, by doing so adding to his legendary reputation for stubbornness. Around 5 o'clock in the morning, a young helicopter crewman comes into his office and hands him a note scrawled on the back of a pad. Martin tells me later: "I will never forget it, the name of the helicopter was Lazy Ace, I think, and the message says, 'The president of the United States directs that Ambassador Martin come out on this helicopter.'"

Martin smiles as he tells me, "Well, what do you do then? Do you try to emulate Admiral Nelson and put your blind eye to the telescope, or you didn't hear it, you didn't get it? For 45 years, I'd been a disciplined officer of the U.S. State Department. I would not sort of spill it all at the end by an act of disobedience. So I got on the chopper and came home."

Around 7:30 a.m., another helicopter, a Sea Knight, swoops low over John F. Kennedy Square (soon to be renamed) and settles on the roof of the embassy. Through binoculars I see a group of Marines running to the open doors of the big ship. It zooms across the city on its way to its carrier offshore. I eventually learn the Marines were part of a security group commanded by Major James Kean, and were temporarily forgotten in the confusion of the evacuation. In 1994, I'll return with Kean and six of the Marines to Saigon for an hourlong interview on the embassy roof, for CNN's "Larry King Live" show. They are astounded to discover on the long-closed building's roof the same sandbags they hid behind as bullets flew while awaiting rescue those many years earlier. And they find the scattered shell casings of the bullets they had used to return sniper fire. They have a lot of unpleasant memories, too, of using Mace and tear gas to hold back the

Vietnamese struggling from below to join their escape on the roof.

The sounds of the helicopters are eventually replaced by human voices. Hearing angry shouting, I spot a dozen people in the middle of Lam Son Square arguing over possession of a king-sized bed. The looting of America's abandoned buildings has begun.

Franjola and I walk up past the French Grall Hospital toward the American Embassy. We see a few bodies on the streets, maybe thieves killed by angry citizens, or the thieves' victims. We see a crowd outside the embassy in a mood opposite the anger of the previous day. They are laughing, comparing looted stuff they've dragged out onto the street. A grinning old woman staggers past with a heavy chair. Inside the consulate building a band of smiling locals are trying to smash open a heavy safe with a sledgehammer. Hundreds of looters are inside the embassy itself. In the pantry we find a gap in the wall, and Franjola says to me, "By God, they've even taken the kitchen sink." On a pile of wet documents and broken furniture on the back lawn we find the heavy bronze plaque engraved with the names of the five American servicemen who died in the attack on the building in the opening hours of the Tet Offensive in 1968. Together, we carry it back to the AP office.

Esper insists on manning the office, just as he has done for most of the previous 10 years. He is listening to Saigon Radio in the monitoring room with our interpreter, who soon shouts, "Surrender, it's surrender!" President Duong Van Minh is announcing complete capitulation; it's now official that South Vietnam is being delivered to the communists. Esper rushes to the teleprinter room and messages New York, and soon receives the satisfying news that AP is five minutes ahead of the UPI news agency with the surrender story. In war or peace, the wire services place a premium on competition.

Esper is looking gaunt, his eyes burning with exhaustion. He hasn't left the office in days, and now he decides to take a walk around outside. Within a few minutes he is back, pale and disturbed. Esper explains that while strolling across nearby Lam Son Square he was approached by a distraught Vietnamese police lieutenant colonel in full uniform, a man he later identifies as Nguyen Van Long, who mutters to him, "It's finished." The officer then walks away about 10 feet, makes a sharp about-face, salutes a nearby statue commemorating Vietnamese infantrymen and raises a .45-caliber pistol. He blows his brains out. For a second George thought he was to be the target. He writes the story with shaky hands.

Franjola has been doing the rounds. He returns and says he was nearly sideswiped by a jeep careening through the streets. It is packed with laughing, shouting young men wearing black pajamas and waving

Russian rifles. I think, black pajamas, Russian rifles? I rush downstairs to Tu Do, the main street. I hear the roar of heavy engines and look toward the old French cathedral where a convoy of Russian Molotova trucks is approaching. Each is loaded with young North Vietnamese soldiers in battle garb, their green pith helmets tilted back as they peer in wonder at the tall buildings they are passing, probably the first they have ever seen. A few local Vietnamese are standing near me. They are staring, speechless. I see a large communist flag unfurl from a room at the nearby Caravelle Hotel, no doubt secretly sewn by the staff.

I notice a group of South Vietnamese soldiers running down a side street, kicking off their uniforms, tossing their weapons into shop doorways. I run back to the AP office, my heart beating wildly as I scramble up the narrow stairways. In the hallway there are a dozen Vietnamese neighbors who clutch at my clothing and implore me to save them. I push into the office and look across to Esper.

"George," I shout, "Saigon has fallen. Call New York." I check my watch. It's 11:43 a.m. I type up a news bulletin about what I've just seen, and hand it to our Vietnamese telex operator, Tammy. He reads it and rises from his chair in alarm. He's looking at the door. I push him down and order him to send my news bulletin. He does, then bolts out of the office and we never see him again.

Around noontime, Franjola and I walk the city streets. Russian tanks are arriving in greater numbers now. Local people are spilling onto the sidewalks, their fears of catastrophe gone. I see a local soldier in a white T-shirt tear the dog tags from his collar and throw them to the ground. I walk through the open gates of the defense ministry building on Gia Long Street. A South Vietnamese officer is in consultation with several North Vietnamese. He turns to me and says, "No pictures," and I continue shooting. After all, there are new sheriffs in town, and they don't seem to mind.

I meet the Australian cameraman Neil Davis who is walking from the presidential palace. He'd watched North Vietnamese tanks crash through the palace gates. He says President Minh has been arrested and taken away. I return to the office, and soon afterward one of our stringer photographers walks into our office with a North Vietnamese officer and his aide, who are amiable, talkative and appreciative of the snacks we offer them.

Later that afternoon Esper suggests that with international communications still up, I write about my reflections of the final day. I know the AP generally frowns on using the personal impressions of its reporters on its news wires, but I do it anyway. I start punching a telex tape and it winds to the floor as I write. I feed the tape into the transmitter and it chugs its way through the machine. "In 13 years of covering the Vietnam War I never dreamed it would end as it did at noon today. I thought it might end with a political deal like in Laos. Even an Armageddon-type battle with the city left in ruins. But a total surrender followed a short two hours later with a cordial meeting in the AP office in Saigon with an armed and battle-garbed North Vietnamese officer with his aide—and over a warm Coke and stale pound cake at that? That is how the Vietnam War ended for me today."

The tape stops running. I punch a few keys but the machine just coughs a couple of times. I try the key again, no response. The AP wire from Saigon to New York is down—and out. The new authorities have finally pulled the plug.

I call out to Esper, "That's it, George. It's over."

2

ASSIGNMENT TO SAIGON

I T'S A RAINY AFTERNOON in June 1962 when I arrive in Saigon, my worldly possessions packed in two beat-up suitcases. I'm grateful for the Saigon job. At 27 years old and on my second year with The Associated Press, I'd worried that my career was all washed up after I was expelled from Indonesia by local officials angry over my forceful reporting. My employers trust me enough to send me to a story of far greater interest to the AP's nearly 2,000 newspaper clients.

I am a small-statured person, and some suggest that I compensate for it with a pugnacious attitude. Maybe so, but I have learned in the years I've been a reporter that a shrinking violet doesn't get the story.

The tree-lined streets, outdoor cafés and striking French provincial architecture of Saigon still earn it the "Pearl of the Orient" label popular during the many years of French colonial control. It's a much more Americanized city than others in Southeast Asia, with young, crew-cut military advisers on leave in civilian clothes crowding the bars and hotels.

Although I arrive under the impression that this country is being sucked inescapably into a war, it turns out that whole families of Americans are settling in for long stays. The dependents of the diplomats, senior military personnel, civilian aid agency workers and think-tank consultants, they're arriving by the hundreds from the United States and they are taking over the comfortable homes abandoned by the French middle class a decade earlier. Near my hotel, I see American schoolkids loitering in a bookstore trading comics.

I pick up a pamphlet at the American Embassy that advises the new arrivals to bring necessary items unavailable here, including "card tables with additional round folding tops, seating six or nine, available at Sears, $6.95; ice cream freezer, hand operated, Sears, $10.97; playing cards forbidden to be sold here; picnic equipment with portable ice chests; folding aluminum tables; Thermos jugs; beach umbrella (two and one-half hours to beach)," along with other items.

On the Rue Pasteur, I meet Malcolm Browne, the AP bureau chief, in his tiny office, tapping on an old Remington typewriter. I ask him what's up with all the civilians in town, and he says, "There's a war going on, that's for sure, but the authorities don't want anyone to hear about it. So they pretend things are normal."

Browne is a striking figure, tall, blond hair casually combed, with an engaging smile. Born in New York City, he graduated from Swarthmore College with a chemistry degree and as a draftee in the mid-1950s drove a tank for the U.S. Army in Korea. He was soon assigned to *Stars and Stripes*, the military newspaper, a job that that hooked him on journalism. He was hired to cover South Vietnam for the AP in 1961.

Browne is nobody's fool. He tells me of an incident a few months earlier when, while dining at the riverside Majestic Hotel, he saw a U.S. Navy transport ship docking across the street, its decks packed with Army H-21 workhorse helicopters, popularly known as "flying bananas" because of their unusual shape. He called an embassy aide for official comment because imports of such specialized military equipment are forbidden under the 1954 Geneva Agreements governing the end of the French colonial war. The American official arrived at the restaurant, and stood beside Mal looking across the street. "I don't see anything," the official said, and walked off.

Mal sees my perplexed expression and explains, "That embassy guy would prefer that I didn't report it. America is doing much more here than it publicly admits. The Kennedy administration is attempting to muzzle every American here because of the political fallout from a military program that is turning into a secret war."

"Did you write the story?" I ask Mal.

"Of course," he says, laughing.

A few months earlier Mal had discovered that American pilots were flying combat missions against the communist Vietcong in Skyraider bombers provided to the South Vietnamese as training planes.

He hands me a pamphlet he has written, a dozen pages of copy paper stapled together, covering subjects ranging from field gear and war coverage survival tips to the artful handling of inside news sources, both Vietnamese and American. It is Browne's manual for successfully covering a secret war. If the military had anything similar it would be classified!

This is the best journalism instruction I have ever received, I tell myself as I read it. The most inspiring passage is Browne's definition of a war reporter's role. "The job for the newsman, as we see it, is simply to cover all the news as fairly and as completely as possible. Our concern is not what effect a given piece of news will have on the public. Our concern is to get the news before the public, in the belief that a free public must be an informed public. The only cause for which a correspondent must fight is to tell the truth and the whole truth."

I am aware that the name Saigon is just beginning to register with an American public more familiar with datelines like Havana and West Berlin and Seoul on critical foreign policy issues. News from the

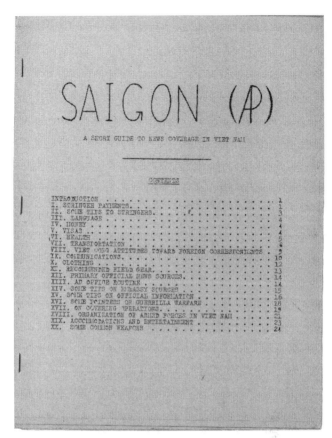

SAIGON (AP)

A SHORT GUIDE TO NEWS COVERAGE IN VIET NAM

CONTENTS

The cover (page i of 25) of The Associated Press Short Guide to News Coverage in Vietnam for staffers and stringers covering the Vietnam War, composed in January 1963 by AP Saigon Bureau Chief Malcolm Browne (1931–2012). The 25-page primer, originally written for Horst Faas and Peter Arnett, provides detailed guidance on all aspects of war coverage, including how to move with troops, how to discern accurate information from propaganda and, most importantly, how to stay safe. (AP Photo/ AP Corporate Archives)

21

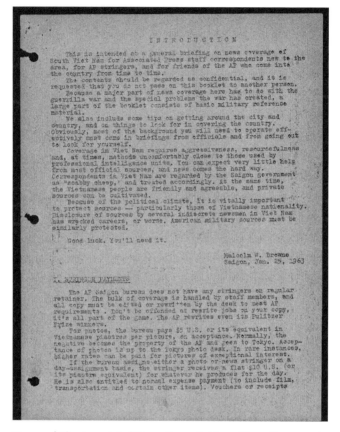

Page 1 of The Associated Press Short Guide to News Coverage in Vietnam, dated Jan. 25, 1963. It advises:

...Coverage in Viet Nam requires aggressiveness, resourcefulness, and, at times, methods uncomfortably close to those used by professional intelligence units. You can expect very little help from most official sources, and news comes the hard way....

Good luck. You'll need it.

(AP Photo/AP Corporate Archives)

capital of a small Southeast Asian country half a world away is evoking little interest among Americans who would identify the Soviet Union as the prime offender in the Cold War. And the troubles of a beleaguered band of young journalists are hardly likely to make the headlines.

An international peace conference in Geneva in 1954 gave North Vietnam to the communists after the conclusive defeat of French colonial forces at Dien Bien Phu earlier that year. The status of the south was left in doubt. The administration of President Dwight Eisenhower removed any doubt where America stood by authorizing some public and much clandestine support for the survival of South Vietnam as an independent, pro-American state.

John F. Kennedy inherited a worsening political and military situation in South Vietnam when he became president in 1961. The country was threatened by an active communist insurgency amongst the rural population and was poorly governed by a Vietnamese family hierarchy that was losing support not only of the population, but also of the American diplomats and military officials who had originally put it in power.

Playing for time, Kennedy sent Vice President Lyndon Baines Johnson to Saigon to explain that South Vietnam was essential to American policy. In an over-the-top endorsement, Johnson publicly described

President Ngo Dinh Diem as "not only the George Washington, the father of your country, but the Franklin Roosevelt as well," and declared that success in Vietnam would keep the United States from having to fight the communists "on the beaches of Hawaii."

At the same time, a worried Secretary of State Dean Rusk told Ambassador Frederick Nolting as he left to take up his post in Saigon in 1961 that "the way things are going out there we'll be lucky if we still have a mission in Saigon six months from now," a comment Nolting mentions in his autobiography.

At a White House meeting, the president told Nolting that he backed the Saigon government, and, as Nolting told me later, "the outcome of your mission depends on finding out for us what kind of man Diem is." But Kennedy was already toying with the idea of a military solution, initially cloaked as a counterinsurgency effort but rapidly emerging into the open as an American war plan.

Ambassador Nolting campaigned to convince Washington that Diem was worthy of support but he was unexpectedly challenged by the visit of an influential figure who had formerly championed the Vietnamese leader's abilities. In the first week of December 1962, I'm invited to meet with that visitor, Senate Majority Leader Mike Mansfield, at his suite at the downtown Caravelle Hotel. My colleague Malcolm

Browne is there, along with David Halberstam of *The New York Times* and Neil Sheehan of UPI.

Mansfield and his aides insist on assuming the role of reporters, questioning us voluminously on our impressions of the situation and revealing their own ambivalence about American policy. Ambassador Nolting later complains that our critical observations unduly colored the delegation's negative assessment of South Vietnam—especially Mansfield's opinion, expressed to President Kennedy, that Diem had wasted the $2 billion that America had spent there. But we were simply telling the Senate visitors things we'd been writing for our news organizations.

3

THE FIRST BIG BATTLE

JUST THREE BLOCKS separate the AP bureau from the military censor's office at the post and telegraph building in the square opposite the old Roman Catholic cathedral, and I walk quickly, trying to suppress my sense of anticipation. I am holding a four-page news story, the first substantial account of the war that I have written since my arrival a few weeks earlier. It is about my three days with the U.S. Marine Corps' 163rd helicopter squadron recently assigned to the Mekong Delta town of Soctrang. They're a friendly bunch, and the commander, Colonel Robert Rathbun, provides a tent for my use. The outfit's mission is to ferry South Vietnamese troops in and out of action in the nearby mangrove swamps that are a stronghold of Vietcong guerrillas.

At the censor's office I hand my story over to a young uniformed Vietnamese officer, who glances briefly at me before taking it carefully in his hand and laying it on his desk. I can sense his distaste.

He takes up a fountain pen with a thick nib that bleeds black ink on the typewritten onionskin pages each time he strikes out a line. He strikes out many lines, 18 of the 23 lines on the first page, 16 on page two, all of page three and 13 lines on page four. He carefully stamps each page with a large official seal that he signs with a flourish, approval for the communication clerks at the post office to send out what's left of my story. He hands the pages back to me with a tight smile. I turn and leave. My story is dead in the water.

American officials in Saigon and Washington publicly insist they have no role in censorship of the western media in South Vietnam. No, they leave it to their Vietnamese allies.

You don't question the censor around here. No explanations. I assume that my story had too much information about American military men enthusiastically helping Vietnamese troops fight their war, too much detail about how difficult the task was against an implacable enemy. Both American and Vietnamese officials prefer to downplay all these points.

I attend airport departure parties for two popular reporters expelled for upsetting the authorities. François Sully of *Newsweek*, who knows Vietnam well, reported that the increasing American undertaking is beginning to mirror the failed efforts of the French forces a decade earlier. Jim Robinson of NBC, an experienced reporter, mentioned in a story that President Diem is a boring interview. I sign a telegram sent by the Saigon press corps to President Kennedy to intervene in such expulsions, to no avail.

At a press conference in Saigon, Admiral Harry D. Felt, the commander in chief of American Pacific forces, bridles at a question I ask about the increasing combat role of American soldiers sent here as advisers. He snarls at me, "Get on the team," the comment later quoted by historian Stanley Karnow in his book "Vietnam, A History," to show how officials wanted reporters to emphasize the positive. AP headquarters advises us that Washington is becoming highly critical of our reporting from Saigon and wonders why our stories are "about 180 degrees" from briefings given AP reporters at the Pentagon and State Department.

I talk to Mal Browne about the state of play. He says that we should report anything that we see, including arms shipments, troop deployments and operational activities, because "if we can see them, so can the enemy." And we should quote informants whom we consider reliable "because they are the experts who know what's going on better than we do."

Very soon I'll recall Mal's advice at an isolated community in the Mekong Delta fringed with palm trees, where water buffalos outnumber humans and rice fields stretch to the horizon. In Vietnamese, its name is Ap Bac. Translated the name means northern hamlet, but in the history of the American war it means turning point.

Our office phone rings, the sound harsher than usual because I'm still getting over a lengthy New Year celebration. It is Jan. 3, 1963. I pick up the phone and hear the voice of a crew chief friend from an American Army Aviation company based at Tan Son Nhut airport. He's breathless with the news that eight U.S. helicopters operating with South Vietnamese forces south of Saigon have been hit, with a least four crewmen wounded. I drive to the airport in my newly acquired white Karmann Ghia sports car, an inexpensive luxury purchased from a Chinese businessman down on his luck. I talk with pilots of helicopters returning from the mission.

I learn that 14 of the 15 American helicopters participating in the operation were hit with a devastating wall of ground fire from concealed communist guerrillas at Ap Bac. Five of the ships are down. Three Americans are dead, two of them crewman and the third an Army captain advising the ground troops. I'm told maybe 100 Vietnamese soldiers are dead. I phone the information to Browne.

He picks up the phone to call our Tokyo bureau that has direct communications with New York. He sees that this story is worth risking bypassing censorship, that the battle may well erase any doubt that America is at war in Vietnam, and it is a story that must be told. Browne begins dictating, "In the costliest defeat for the American support effort in Vietnam, communist gunners today shot five American helicopters from the sky and turned back hundreds of South Vietnamese soldiers attempting to capture a tiny hamlet in the Mekong Delta." Browne's story hits the front pages of America's newspapers. Our New York editors demand a quick follow-up story.

I figure that the authorities will close all access to Ap Bac, or try to. I call a reporter friend from *Stars and Stripes*, Steve Stibbens, who often hangs out at our office, and I ask him to help. Next morning, Steve arrives at our office in his U.S. Marine uniform, and David Halberstam of *The New York Times* and I climb in behind him in his jeep. We head south down Route 1 into the Mekong Delta. Halberstam and I try to look suitably official as our driver negotiates military roadblocks and checkpoints with a smile and a salute, his uniform his passkey.

Beyond the province capital of Tan An, we bounce over a muddy track to an airstrip alongside a flooded paddy field at Tan Hiep. There is chaos. Trucks and jeeps, engines running, compete for space at the edge of the small runway where Vietnamese soldiers watch as helicopters come and go. I see a familiar face, Colonel Daniel Boone Porter, amongst the American and Vietnamese officers who seem to be arguing with each other.

Porter is the senior American adviser for the delta region. Friendly in previous visits, he is unhappy today. He tells me that at Ap Bac for the first time the Vietcong guerrillas have stood their ground and fought back when attacked by government troops, fighting strongly rather that striking quickly and melting away into the countryside. Porter shakes his head and says, "We had superior forces and superior firepower. We advisers were hoping for a confrontation like this to prove that our tactics would work. They didn't."

Halberstam and I hitch a ride on an American helicopter that is surveying the battlefield. Down below is a scene of carnage. We see dead bodies in the mud. Bits of downed helicopters are strewn in the rice fields. Deep tracks on the ground lead to the wreckage of armored personal carriers destroyed in the fighting. The village itself is in ruins. In all, 65 government troops were killed in addition to the American dead. The Vietcong slipped away during the night, dragging their own dead with them.

Returning to Tan Hiep, I see an honor guard drawn up for senior officers, including General Paul D. Harkins, in charge of the U.S. Military Assistance Command, an impressive-looking veteran of World War II. He is usually impatient with reporters. I ask him what is happening and he says with a straight face, "We've got the Vietcong in a trap and we're going to spring it in half an hour," and he turns away.

I seek out an American officer, Lieutenant Colonel John Paul Vann, whom I know to be a straight shooter. He is the senior adviser to the Vietnamese 7th Division that launched the Ap Bac operation. Vann is a wiry, compact Texan with a hair-trigger temper and a reputation for bravery. He invites Halberstam and me to talk out of earshot of the others. Vann is very angry.

He ridicules General Harkins's statement of a few minutes earlier. He launches into a fierce attack on the performance of the Vietnamese soldiers he had been advising for months. "It's a damn shame," he says, that such a debacle could happen after all the efforts by the United States to equip and advise them.

Vann is red-faced now, stamping his feet and drawing the attention of bystanders some distance away. The Vietcong are escaping, and the Vietnamese officers he is advising don't seem to care. Vann's answer, he tells me, is to mobilize his own 60-man American advisory staff, the office workers, the cooks, the maintenance staff and the drivers, led by his military advisory team. "We'll get 'em ourselves if the Vietnamese can't do it," Vann exclaims as he walks away to issue orders.

I return to Saigon that evening and file my detailed story to New York via phone call to the Tokyo bureau. Again we bypass censorship. A few of our colleagues have been expelled for doing much less, but I figure that with all of the resident western press corps filing

Ap Bac stories the same way as we did, the government will be hard-pressed to punish us all.

AP New York congratulates us on our enterprise and advises that our stories on Ap Bac have received smash play in America's newspapers. I sense that our eyewitness reports from this distant Cold War outpost will raise less concern from our superiors in the future.

Saigon youths join Provisional Revolutionary Government (PRG) troops on May 4, 1975, waving weapons and PRG flags on Tu Do Street in Saigon, Vietnam. (AP Photo/Matt Franjola)

North Vietnamese troops in the AP Saigon bureau, Apr. 30, 1975, describe their route into the city to Matt Franjola, Peter Arnett, George Esper, and an unidentified AP staffer. (AP Photo/Sarah Errington)

A North Vietnamese tank rolls through the gate of the Presidential Palace in Saigon on Apr. 30, 1975, signifying the fall of South Vietnam. (AP Photo)

Provisional Revolutionary Government (PRG) forces enter Saigon and are seen parked outside the Independence Palace on Apr. 30, 1975, minutes after the unconditional surrender of Vietnam. (AP Photo)

Defeated South Vietnam President Duong Van Minh (middle) walks out of Independence Palace after surrendering to PRG forces in Saigon on May 1, 1975. (AP Photo)

Celebration in Hanoi of the final victory of North Vietnam over South Vietnam. Several thousand marchers filled in the square in front of the Opera house carrying banderoles on May 2, 1975. (AP Photo)

More than ten thousand people gather in front of Independence Palace in the biggest rally since the PRG takeover of Saigon to attend a ceremony where the Saigon Military Administrative Committee is introduced on May 7, 1975. (AP Photo/Manh Hung)

4

TESTS OF FIRE

GIA LONG PALACE looms ahead as I walk along streets flying red and yellow bunting and past ice cream parlors busy with the celebrating crowds. I'll soon have my first look at the small, plump man chosen to be ruler in Saigon at a time when the country is falling to pieces, a man reputed to laugh rarely though today, in a neat dark suit pulled tight around his middle, he smiles a lot. Ngo Dinh Diem is observing the eighth anniversary of his presidency of South Vietnam, defying the odds against his survival that was initially put at six months by some experts. Eight years have gone by, and the bombing attacks and attempted coups d'état against him have come and gone.

He nods at me as I shuffle along the receiving line. His jet-black hair seems lacquered on. Diem was chosen to lead his country because of impressive nationalist credentials and stubborn courage in stabilizing the south after the French war, but he's becoming an odd man out for leading the fast-developing life-or-death struggle against the communists. Even Ambassador Frederick Nolting, his most fervent American supporter, acknowledges Diem's eccentricities and Mandarin style, remembering sitting through six hours of "incredible verbosity" in his first private meeting with him. "Between us," Nolting writes in his autobiography, "we must have smoked several packs of Vietnamese cigarettes and drank dozens of cups of pale, lukewarm tea."

General Maxwell D. Taylor, sent several times to Saigon as an emissary of President Kennedy, tells me in an interview that he noticed Diem "at times getting a glassy look in his eyes and dozing off," during his presentations. William Colby, chief of station for the CIA, says in an interview Diem sees his function "as a kind of monk to bring his mission to an end, to bring Vietnam into the modern world." Kennedy's impatience with Diem's modus operandi is said to have persuaded him to pursue a military option that will place South Vietnam's future more under American supervision.

In mid-February 1963, I sit through a speech given by Ambassador Nolting at a business conference praising Diem and renewing his displeasure with the press, and calling for an end to "idle criticism, from snide remarks and unnecessary comments, and from spreading allegations and rumors which either originate from communist sources, or play directly into communist hands." I feel we're covering Saigon like our stateside colleagues are covering Washington, D.C., and too bad that the ambassador doesn't like it. I don't know how not to write stories about what we are seeing and hearing.

In the early morning of June 11, Mal Browne, our bureau chief at AP, is roused from his sleep with a telephone tip from a monk friend at the Xa Loi pagoda, the center of a growing Buddhist protest against the Saigon government. An important demonstration will wind through city streets an hour or so later. Such events have become commonplace, but Browne and office assistant Bill Havantran attend anyway because the continuing Buddhist unrest that began with the bloody police suppression of a religious parade in Hue on May 8 has caught the attention of American editors.

Police are clearing the streets of traffic. A group of monks march silently and slowly along Phan Dinh Phuong Avenue behind an old gray sedan. They stop in front of the Cambodian Embassy. A few monks step out of the ranks as the others, several hundred in number, form a circle in the middle of the inter-section. Browne and Havantran ready their cameras. Something new is about to happen.

An elderly monk in bright yellow robes walks slowly from the sedan and seats himself cross-legged on a cushion. Two companions pour gasoline over his shaved head and drench his robes. The monk lights a match in his lap and then folds his hands in the lotus position as flames envelop him. An astonished Browne clicks away as another monk in the crowd shouts out in English, "This is the Buddhist flag. He died for this flag. Thich Quang Duc burned for this flag."

Browne's photograph of the aged monk enveloped in smoke and flames shocks the world. Later, Browne is sometimes asked why he didn't intervene and prevent the suicide. His response: "I was too busy doing my job, but there were several hundred militant monks there. They would have torn me to pieces if I made a move," he told one interviewer.

The ramifications of that one picture are immediate. President Kennedy has a copy of the front page of *The Washington Post* on his desk in the Oval Office when he meets with Henry Cabot Lodge, who has agreed to replace Nolting as ambassador. Kennedy points to the picture and instructs, "Get out there and make sure this doesn't happen again," Lodge tells me in an interview.

The Saigon government clamps down harder on the Buddhists and their sympathizers. One afternoon I see two truckloads of young girls dressed in traditional silken white ao dai dresses being driven from their high school dormitories to detention centers because of their Buddhist sympathies. Browne is accused by Madame Ngo Dinh Nhu, the firebrand sister-in-law of President Diem, of providing the gasoline for Thich Quang Duc's immolation.

The police crack down ferociously on our news coverage. On July 7, I cover a demonstration at the Chantareansay pagoda in the northern suburbs of Saigon. I'm pushed into an alley by surging protesters. I try to get my bearings as I'm punched in the head. I'm tackled to the ground and beaten up and kicked by a group of plainclothes security men who stamp on my camera. They are enjoying it. Suddenly a large person is standing over me, growling like a bear, his fists raised. It is my buddy David Halberstam of *The New York Times*, who is built like a fullback. He pulls me to my feet and turns to my much smaller attackers and says loudly, "You want him? Then get through me." I doubt the security men understood his words, but they did his menace. They raised their hands in submission and slipped away.

The local authorities up the ante. Two days later, Browne and I are ordered to the main Saigon police station on trumped-up charges of assaulting the police, and subject to a four-hour interrogation that borders on the Kafkaesque in its disorienting and menacing quality. We are freed after word reaches the American Embassy that we might face serious charges that would further heighten the already fraught situation and become a cause célèbre.

By now our troubles have caught the attention of the media establishment in America. Our New York headquarters advises us of a letter sent to President Kennedy on July 18 by the president of the American Society of Newspaper Editors, Herbert Drucker, editor of *The Hartford Courant*. It says in part, "In recent weeks as you are aware there have been charges that Vietnamese secret police pummeled, knocked down and kicked American reporters and smashed their cameras." He concludes the letter, "It is not yet certain that all possible efforts are being made to prevent further deliberate obstacles to free reporting. Whatever the difficulties, we urge you to bear in mind the need for the American people to have the fullest possible factual information from South Vietnam, no matter what anyone may think is right or wrong about the situation there."

I feel the wind in my sails. The bruises, the arrests, the hectoring by officials are nothing compared to my growing awareness that I'm doing the right thing, that I, Browne and the other reporters have consequential roles to play in the growing drama that is South Vietnam.

I'm at the airport to cover the arrival of Ambassador Henry Cabot Lodge, scion of a prominent Massachusetts family, a legendary figure in American diplomacy and politics. I ride there with my colleagues in a bus escorted by police through streets emptied by the early curfew. We expect Lodge's appointment to be a game changer, with pressure put on Ngo Dinh Diem to allow political freedoms and to improve military competence. Halberstam and Neil Sheehan, both well versed in New England patrician ways, joke that in the challenging days ahead for American-Vietnamese relations, "Our old Mandarin can lick your old Mandarin."

Lodge did not disappoint. He emerged from his aircraft into glaring television lights and began talking about American democracy and the essential role of the press. Four newsmen on the flight with him include the AP's chief executive in Asia, Robert Eunson. He pulls me out of the crowd and says, "The ambassador's on our side," introducing me to one of Lodge's aides, Major John Michael Dunn, who nods in affirmation.

I'm exhilarated. Unlike his predecessor Frederick Nolting, the State Department veteran, who always seemed impatient with the press and regularly swatted at us as though we were flies buzzing around carrion, Lodge is an old pol, a former candidate for the vice presidency of the United States among many other political offices, and in his early life a journalist. He knows the value of a friendly media.

Within a few hours of his arrival on Aug. 22, 1963, Lodge makes a well-publicized visit to two Buddhist monks granted asylum at the U.S. military headquarters on Rue Pasteur. On Nov. 1, 71 days later, the Saigon government is overthrown in a brutal coup d'état by disaffected military officers. President Diem and his influential brother Ngo Dinh Nhu are both murdered after surrendering.

Flashing forward 15 years, it's early autumn 1978, and I sit with an aging Lodge in his family home in Boston. As amiable as always, he's agreed to a television interview for a documentary I'm working on. He tells me about the day Diem died.

"I visited his palace late morning along with General Harkins and Admiral Felt. I was leaving for Washington on a routine visit the following day. Diem says, 'Every time the American ambassador goes to Washington I hear coup rumors. I hear these rumors now, I know there will be a coup but I don't know who's behind it.' I took Harkins and Felt home to lunch, and while we're sitting there we hear this tremendous automatic weapons fire, it sounded as though it was right in the next room. And the planes were flying overhead. It was the beginning of the overthrow."

I ask Lodge what he knew in advance, because the Pentagon Papers, the U.S. government's secret study of the war, had already revealed American awareness of the plotting. The old Mandarin smiled. "President Kennedy told us to stay out of it, let it run its course. He wanted the Vietnamese to run it as a Vietnamese thing. And Washington said they would stay out of it and they stayed out of it."

5

REPORTING LBJ'S WIDENING WAR

THE FALLOUT from the murders of two presidents, Ngo Dinh Diem and John F. Kennedy, just weeks apart in November 1963 is plunging South Vietnam into a political and military tailspin that seriously undermines America's 10 years of nation building.

The Vietnamese generals who successfully conspired to overthrow their president are becoming popular celebrities, enjoying their success in the nightclubs of Saigon and inviting the American press corps to party with them. But squabbling behind closed doors over the choice of a successor ends not with equanimity but with the seizure of power in late January by a young field commander, General Nguyen Khanh, who arrests the others and expresses a fierce anti-communism.

U.S. President Lyndon Johnson is determined to provide strong support to South Vietnam and, as he says to an aide, "not be the first American president to lose a war." Even though American Embassy officials see the goateed General Khanh as a lightweight, Johnson has little choice but to give his official approval to the new regime, as he does to the nine successor governments and juntas that pass through Saigon in the next 19 months of political upheaval.

The communist insurgents ratchet up their war tactics with bold frontal attacks against formerly secure targets, taking immediate advantage of the disarray spreading in the South Vietnamese military as officers loyal to the previous regime are purged and as provincial officials are replaced.

In less than five years, the shadowy communist organization called the South Vietnam National Liberation Front expands from a handful of members to a position of America's No. 1 shooting enemy, known as the Vietcong. It has grown to an estimated 300,000 active members. Occasional front supporters may number 4 to 5 million.

The widening war has many fronts, and with little or no cooperation from officials it is difficult for reporters to cover because we are barred for the time being from riding helicopters into battle areas. I settle on a practical if unorthodox approach. When I hear rumors of significant actions, I watch for the early morning airlifts of soldiers out of the Tan Son Nhut helicopter base and determine the general direction. I give chase in my Karmann Ghia automobile along the main highways as long as the helicopters are in view above me. I then take side roads to where I anticipate there is action. I keep trying until I see bodies of soldiers on the road and wounded being treated. My arrival in a white sports car invariably causes more incredulity than alarm, and I usually get the story.

My companion on these adventures is often our photographer Horst Faas, a beefy, amiable German with a steely determination to shoot the most explicit photos of the war. Horst often works alone.

On a late spring afternoon the door of our Saigon office bursts open and Horst comes in. His shirt and trousers are muddied, his hair ruffled. He explains that he's been riding with a Vietnamese armored cavalry troop on the Plain of Reeds, a desolate place at the southern tip of the country dominated by the communists. An American adviser in Horst's vehicle called in airstrikes on a village to prevent guerrillas escaping, causing civilian casualties.

Thirty minutes later, Horst comes out from our toilet that serves as his darkroom. He is holding a bunch of damp black-and-white prints. He lays them on a table with the comment, "It's the worst I've seen in three wars." They show horrible things, the civilian losses in sharp focus. In one photo, a farmer clasps his 2-year-old son in his arms, the child's clothes burned off by napalm, his scorched skin hanging. In another photo, a peasant holds the body of a similarly disfigured child up to soldiers, who peer indifferently from the top of an armored personnel carrier. Other pictures are equally upsetting.

By chance we are being visited by the general manager and chief executive of The Associated Press, Wes Gallagher. It takes a lot to shock him, a veteran newsman chosen by the nation's most important newspaper, television and radio owners to run AP, the cooperative that is the basic news provider to much of America. Although Horst's pictures shock him, Gallagher allows us to distribute them, anyway.

But he tells me, "Every picture editor in America will want to know how such a thing could happen when American servicemen are involved." He says we must present the context, noting that government officials in Washington may accuse us of bias. I write an accompanying story pointing out instances of communist atrocities and observing that with both sides building up their arsenals the war has entered a new phase of violence and brutality. Napalm, the jellied gasoline that spreads a wall of fire on exploding, is in routine use.

Gallagher has some important information for us. He senses from his contacts in Washington, D.C., that President Johnson is more likely than the slain President Kennedy was to send American combat troops to fight in South Vietnam. Accordingly, he is planning to beef up our bureau with more permanent staffers.

A distinguished reporter in World War II, Gallagher offers me some friendly advice for the future. "Get along with the generals and the top sergeants and be polite and you'll do fine. It's your personal demeanor they will judge you on, and not your stories." I respect Gallagher's opinions as much as I am impressed with his striking bearing. But as for his advice? Well, I'd tried that already in Saigon, and it didn't work.

Gallagher is prescient. Lyndon Johnson does indeed commit American combat troops to South Vietnam, in March of 1965, when it becomes clear South Vietnam's military forces are being defeated on the battlefield. With the arriving Marines and Army units comes a swarm of reporters and photographers from newspapers and television networks.

Also in the mix: an accompanying cadre of military officers and civilian officials intent on shaping the news coverage to the needs of the Johnson administration. In earlier wars, strict censorship on the battlefield molded the message to the home public. The Johnson administration, already meeting criticism at home about the fighting, is unwilling to admit that the commitment to Vietnam is as consequential as earlier conflicts.

Meanwhile, Gallagher declares a war of his own, criticizing political interference in reporting foreign wars. In a speech to a group of newspaper editors in

1965, he observes that government officials frequently cite what they call "the national interest" in trying to discourage the reporting of unpleasant news from Vietnam and other troubled areas. He asserts, "We are not a vehicle to serve 'the national interest' as defined by politicians, but to publish the truth as we see it."

I am invariably polite to the arriving American officers and soldiers that I cover, as Gallagher has suggested, and I'm not a confrontational person, anyway. That is not being said about my reporting. The commanding officer of the U.S. Marine Corps, General Wallace Greene, flatly denies an exclusive story I write on Aug. 20, 1965, about a column of mechanized Marines badly mauled during the first amphibious landing of the war.

The mission of Supply Column 21 is to reinforce a Marine battalion farther inland, but the swampy paddy fields bog down three of the heavy armored vehicles. Concealed communist soldiers dressed in black pajama uniforms and camouflaged helmets rise out of hedges and swamps, close enough to lob hand grenades and fire anti-tank shells at the stranded Marines. The terraced paddy fields make maneuvering difficult for the two tracked vehicles still mobile, and when one is knocked out the survivors lock themselves in the remaining one. When I step off a rescue helicopter with photographer Tim Page we see American bodies half submerged in the swamps and badly wounded Marines desperate for medical attention. As we try to help, the survivors tell us their stories, of the death struggles of brave young men, of the fear of injury or capture as projectiles slam against the only shelter they have. I file my story that evening with my photographs. Newspapers play it big, some using many of the photos, because of the premonition of things to come.

Marine Corps spokesmen insist on the broader success of the mission, to secure territory to the south of the planned air base at Chu Lai. Officially, Supply Column 21's travails never happened. General Greene's criticism is so damaging that Gallagher invites him to a conference at AP headquarters in New York. He shows him all my pictures. He reads him my story. The general finally believes.

Months later the AP sends me a letter written by Corporal Frank Guilford of Philadelphia, one of the Marines I quoted. He writes that my story had worried his wife but that he was glad I had arrived at the scene and written my account "because American soldiers are not receiving enough credit for their sacrifice in Vietnam."

My Marine story foretells the struggle American soldiers will have in the heavily populated rice farming regions in South Vietnam, where local communist guerrillas fight to defend their villages. I write a series of stories a few months later portending the greater struggle American forces would face against North Vietnamese regular troops in the border regions where 300-foot-high triple-canopy jungles and high mountains define the battlefields.

I see Neil Sheehan, formerly my UPI competitor and now with *The New York Times*, boarding a transport plane for Pleiku in the early hours of Nov. 15, 1965, at Saigon's Tan Son Nhut airport. We are heading for the same location, a remote battle scene hundreds of miles away in the mountains along the Cambodian border. We've heard the same sketchy reports that the first major battle between American troops and the North Vietnamese army is raging in a place called Ia Drang.

We hitch a jeep ride to the Pleiku base of the U.S. 1st Cavalry Division's 3rd Brigade, and watch medical evacuation helicopters arriving with wounded soldiers. We ride back with one of them to the pickup point, a cramped landing zone called X-Ray hidden among the trees in the Ia Drang valley. We see organized mayhem. Wounded are being carried on stretches to our helicopter. We hear shouts of "incoming" as shells explode nearby. I see Joe Galloway, a reporter from UPI running toward the chopper we have just left. He throws a thumbs-up as he clambers aboard and heads off to file his exclusive stories of the first day's battle.

There is still plenty for Sheehan and me to see. I find Lieutenant Colonel Hal Moore, the commander of the embattled unit, the 1st Battalion of the 7th Cavalry Regiment, squatting beside a tree and barking orders into his phone. He confirms that the communist attack is continuing, and he's identified the North Vietnamese 304th Infantry Division as one of the enemy units. He worries that one of his infantry companies is missing behind enemy lines. He's calling for more ammunition. He doesn't have much time to talk with me, but he's already said enough. I join a patrol probing enemy positions through the tree lines to the west. I interview wounded soldiers waiting for rescue. By late afternoon I leave to file my story from a communication center at Pleiku and return in the morning with photographer Rick Merron.

The stubborn bravery of the cavalrymen at landing zone X-Ray was well worthy of acclaim, and the American high command quickly proclaimed it a great victory. But more was to come. On Nov. 17, the North Vietnamese ambushed and overran a marching column of the 2nd Battalion of the 7th Cavalry in the same area. Of the 500 Americans in the column, 150 were killed, 50 wounded and only 84 could be immediately returned to action. My colleague Merron interviewed the survivors, who told harrowing tales of the brutal slaughter, with the hidden enemy jumping down from trees to attack, and soldiers fleeing in panic.

The commander of American Forces in Vietnam, General William C. Westmoreland, preferred the narrative of glorious victory to any suggestion of defeat. He phoned our bureau chief, Edwin White, and demanded that we stop interviewing "ordinary soldiers in battle because they are not in a position to see the big picture and may be emotionally affected by the action." White tells me to ignore the call. Westmoreland did not have a veto power on what we wrote. To me, the point of view of the ordinary soldier was the key to many of my best stories.

Back home in Saigon, the phone beside my bed is ringing in the half light of dawn. The night man in our office is calling. He has a message for me from New York. I've won the Pulitzer Prize for international reporting. That makes three for the AP in three years. Malcolm Browne shared the prize with *The New York Times*'s David Halberstam in 1964; Horst Faas won for photography in 1965, now me in 1966.

My wife, Nina, is awake and questioning. Our son, Andrew, 18 months old, starts bawling. I tell her the news and we hug. I'd married Nina two years earlier after meeting her when she returned to her native Vietnam from a two-year postgraduate course in library science at the University of North Carolina. It was love at first sight for me. Nina puts up with my dangerous professional life, aware that journalists are being killed in combat, including Huynh Thanh My, a talented young Vietnamese AP photographer newly married with a baby on the way, who was killed the previous summer.

Nina understands what it's all about. Her family fled south to Saigon from the communists in 1955. Her brother-in-law is an officer in the South Vietnamese army. I've convinced her journalists have a necessary role to play in telling the truth about war, no matter the risk.

I leave my apartment and walk on clouds down Rue Pasteur to our new office. On the way, I'm stopped by the brilliant *New York Times* correspondent Charles Mohr, who I suspect was also entered in the Pulitzer Prize contest. He shakes my hand and offers to buy me lunch.

Nina and I fly to New York to attend the 50th anniversary celebration of the Pulitzer Prize in the grand ballroom at the Plaza Hotel. We are on the stage with the year's other winners, and I look out to the sparkling black-tie audience filled with as many Pulitzer winners in all categories as the organizers had been able to round up. Afterward, I pose for a photograph with the legendary AP winners from two previous wars. I am the new kid on the block.

Wes Gallagher pulls me aside to tell me that President Johnson has been complaining about my reporting, bringing it up to newspaper editors invited to visit the White House. He says he met with the president.

I try to imagine the standoff between the most powerful man in America and one of the most influential news executives. They are matched physically, with maybe an advantage for Gallagher with his menacing bushy black eyebrows shading piercing gray eyes. Gallagher tells me the conversation.

"Mr. President, I understand you have been critical of some of AP's stories from Vietnam?"

"Oh, no," the president replies, patting Gallagher on the back.

Gallagher: "Well, I just wanted you to know, Mr. President, that the AP is not against you or for you."

The president: "That's not quite the way I like it."

Gallagher pulls me closer. "I want you to keep doing what you're doing, Peter," he says. "But I have a warning. Stick to the facts and the truth at all times. If you make a mistake, even a little one, I can't protect you."

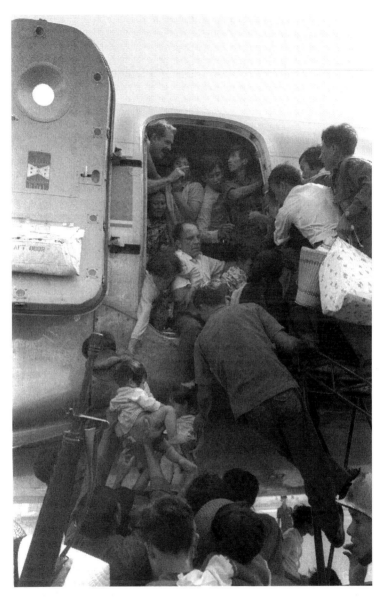

A U.S. civilian pilot in the aircraft doorway tries to maintain order as panicking South Vietnamese civilians scramble to get aboard during evacuation of Nha Trang, Apr. 1, 1975. Thousands of civilians and South Vietnamese soldiers fought for space on the aircraft to Saigon as communist forces advanced following the fall of Qui Nhon, to the north. (AP Photo)

South Vietnamese Marines leap in panic aboard a cutter from an LST in Danang Harbor in Danang, Vietnam, Apr. 1, 1975, as they are evacuated from the city. (AP Photo)

Vietnamese boat people try to escape from Cam Ranh Bay, Vietnam, to a U.S. Navy ship, Feb. 8, 1975. (AP Photo/Nick Ut)

U.S. Navy personnel aboard the USS *Blue Ridge* push a helicopter into the sea off the coast of Vietnam in order to make room for more evacuation flights from Saigon, Apr. 29, 1975. (AP Photo)

Mobs of Vietnamese people scale the wall of the U.S. Embassy in Saigon, trying to get to the helicopter pickup zone, just before the end of the Vietnam War on Apr. 29, 1975. (AP Photo/Neal Ulevich)

Thich Quang Duc, a Buddhist monk, burns himself to death on a Saigon street Jun. 11, 1963, to protest alleged persecution of Buddhists by the South Vietnamese government. (AP Photo/Malcolm Browne)

New York Times reporter David Halberstam, center in glasses, defends bloodied AP reporter Peter Arnett, far left, as plainclothes Saigon police agents beat several members of the Western press corps in a Saigon alleyway, Jul. 7, 1963. (AP Photo/Malcolm Browne)

6

"SEARCH AND DESTROY" UP CLOSE

SUCCESS FOR AMERICAN combat troops in their earliest battles in South Vietnam gives officials confidence that the war can be won quickly. At least that's what they say in public. Secretary of Defense Robert McNamara visits Saigon so often and is so optimistic in his assessments that people begin calling it "McNamara's War." At an airport press conference late in 1965 when I ask him about that, he says, "I'm proud some think that way." Years later, he is quoted as having doubts about victory around the same time he answered my question.

The stated American military strategy is to force the communist enemy to call off the war by killing so many of its soldiers so quickly that it has no choice but to give up. Officials point to the well-publicized battle in the Ia Drang valley in November 1965 between American air cavalry troopers and North Vietnamese regular soldiers as a template. Several hundred elite American soldiers were casualties in that brutal, three-day struggle, but far more North Vietnamese combatants died, according to official estimates, as many as 10-to-1. Such a kill ratio, if true and if maintained, seems to portend an unbeatable outcome. The body count becomes the primary indicator of battlefield success.

Not everyone is so sure. I write an analysis that says even with 180,000 combat troops committed to Vietnam at that time, the United States is losing its edge against the communists. Most American and South Vietnamese troops are pinned down by security jobs—including keeping what they hold—so that surprisingly few battalions are available for searching out the enemy. North Vietnam is pouring its own army into the fight. By early 1966, the battlefield situation has returned to where it was a year earlier, before a surge of new American forces tipped the balance temporarily in the allies' favor.

I try to make friends with Major General William DePuy, the young commander of the renowned "Big Red One," the 1st Infantry Division based near Saigon. DePuy is a favorite of Westmoreland's and worked as a staff officer for the general for two years before being sent to his new command with instructions to "get cracking." DePuy becomes the proponent of a uniquely aggressive tactic labeled "search and destroy," designed to launch massive firepower and troop assaults against confirmed enemy locations to secure the highest body counts.

One day an information officer with the 1st Division phones me with an invitation to visit his headquarters at Di An. DePuy strides into our meeting room. He says he's been reading some of my stories in the military newspaper *Stars and Stripes*. "Arnett, you don't know what the hell you're talking about," he says. "You better stick around with us for a while. This is where it's happening."

I discover that DePuy is a dynamic, demanding leader, and feisty. He's a "bantam rooster" to his men, a fellow officer commenting that that's not a bad way to describe DePuy's "barely contained energy package" in a 5-foot-8-inch body weighing 140 pounds. His intensity frightens his own people as his command becomes infamous in military circles for the high turnover of field officers whose performances he decides are less than tolerable.

While preparing for a field trip with DePuy, I ask him about the criticism and he responds, "I'm interested only in combat effectiveness, not personal feelings or career ambitions. I want only the best." This trip takes us to the 3rd Brigade base at Lai Khe, once a thriving French rubber plantation now hosting 2,000 American soldiers. Our helicopter lands near a line of waiting officers, and DePuy pins a medal on the chest of one of them, Lieutenant Colonel Alexander Haig, a battalion commander being cited for his leadership and heroism at the battle of Ap Gu. Haig's bravery in surviving a helicopter crash in the middle of the battle and joining his troops in hand-to-hand combat with the enemy wins attention in Washington. Within five years, he's a general on the staff of Henry Kissinger. A decade later, he's secretary of state. It's hard to fault DePuy's earlier judgment.

DePuy loves helicopters the way NASCAR drivers of that time love their Fords or Chevys. He's in the sky every day in his UH-1 Huey, hovering over his troops as they tangle with the enemy in villages below and in barely visible battles in the midst of deep jungle, yelling instructions over his field phone. His most dramatic tactical innovation is the massing of multiple fleets of helicopters to airlift his soldiers into battle in the communist-controlled wildernesses of War Zones D and C, north and west of his brigade base camps.

Hearing that DePuy's planning a large-scale operation in early summer, I beg to go along. I arrive at the Lai Khe base, one of the launching areas, by driving along "thunder road," the name given to this stretch of Route 13 that is often mined by local communist sympathizers. I learn the operation's name, Birmingham. At dawn the next morning, I see DePuy consulting with his officers at an airstrip crowded with helicopters. Grim-faced soldiers line up outside the doors.

DePuy beckons me over. He is grinning. "I had to twist the old man's arm," he said, referring to Lieutenant General Jonathan Seaman, a popular, mild-mannered officer who is his superior. "But I've got nearly a hundred transport and gunships, and we will launch within the hour." He invites me aboard the command helicopter and hands me earphones. I had written about DePuy's contention that victory in war always favored the side that was able to concentrate its forces at a critical time on the battlefield. This is what he plans on doing today. But it's also a tactic that is a cardinal principle of communist guerrillas, whose units rarely attack unless they field superior forces.

The target areas this day are small clearings in the jungle in War Zone C, named during the earlier French war. In the air now, I twist in my seat. I see helicopters swarming around and behind us like migrating geese in seasonal flight. DePuy is chattering on his command phone as the vastness of the war zone opens up before us, beyond the last vestiges of populated communities. I thrill at being a part of this incredible display of America's military might.

DePuy calls for artillery support, and I see bursts of flame and smoke in the three landing zones he has designated. We fly on, and the artillery shells keep coming, the explosions so near now that I can almost hear them over the roar of the rotor blades. The shells will clear the landing zones of enemy personnel and fortifications. I was an artilleryman in my youth during required military service in my native New Zealand. I'm thinking these shells are flying right over us, maybe closely. DePuy sees my consternation and shouts into his phone, "The trick, Arnett, is in the timing."

Airstrikes from a dozen planes provide a spectacular denouement, splashing napalm and high explosive bombs into the jungle foliage as the first helicopters swing into landing formation and, one by one, hover over the scarred ground, disgorging the troopers and then flying off as the next ship comes in. By midmorning, DePuy has sent more than a thousand of his best troops into an enemy stronghold rarely penetrated in the 15 years of warfare that preceded them.

Flying back to base with DePuy, I see he is elated. He has other units ready to reinforce, he tells me. He can send them into War Zone C at 90 miles an hour. DePuy even suggests that the epic battle at Dien Bien Phu that ended in disaster for the French in 1954 could have been won with his tactics. Maybe. Ultimately, his Birmingham operation will be less successful than expected.

DePuy makes colorful news copy. He likes the story I write on Aug. 31, 1966, that calls him a military genius who would either kill all the communists in his division area north of Saigon or they would kill him. He makes the cover of *Newsweek* magazine on

Dec. 5, 1966. But there is a downside to his tactical boldness. To save his soldiers' lives he orders that in making contact with the enemy they avoid being decisively engaged. Better to call in air and artillery fire while support units maneuver. By keeping American soldiers out of the kill zone while making maximum use of firepower, DePuy does indeed save his own men, but there is a disproportionate loss of civilian lives and property that alarms the high command and clouds his career.

I interview General DePuy in Washington a few years after the war. He has regained his reputation as one of the brightest officers in the military, widely seen as the chief architect of the restructuring of American army doctrine after the withdrawal from Vietnam. I ask him about "search and destroy," and he says he regrets the title. "It started out with the best of intentions," he tells me, "to search for the enemy, find him and destroy him. Later I guess it became associated with pictures of troops searching villages and setting them on fire. It came to suggest we were destroying the whole country."

Airlifting soldiers into battle by helicopter is one thing. What they face on the ground is another. AP photographer Horst Faas and I accept an invitation to cover a risky infantry action west of Saigon. The mission is to rout out communist snipers from tunnels and bunkers in the tangle of wild rubber trees and shrub bordering Cu Chi, a town on the main highway to the Cambodian border. The invitation is extended by an officer we see as a friend, Lieutenant Colonel George Eyster, commander of the renowned Black Lion battalion, the 2nd of the 28th Regiment, 1st Infantry Division. Eyster is a tall quiet man whom we often run into in our visits to his brigade base. He's a West Point graduate and modest about his lineage; his father was a brigadier general and chief information officer for American forces in Europe in World War II. He lives in Cocoa Beach, Florida, and enjoys showing us pictures of his wife and kids.

We arrive at the operational area at night, and move out at dawn. Eyster and a company commander, Captain George Dailey, decide to go on foot along the visible paths and tracks in the scrub to better bring up jeep-mounted weaponry. They admit it's a gamble because snipers might be observing us from concealed tunnels.

An hour into the mission I join Eyster, Dailey and a radio operator to peer at a detailed operational map of the area. Eyster is pointing to a map location just ahead when four shots ring out in a cluster, echoing loudly through the undergrowth. My shoulder is next to Eyster's, and I feel his body shake. I hear him gasp. He slides to the ground, as I do next to him for my own safety. "George, I'm hit," he mutters to Dailey, who is now on his feet shouting, "The colonel's hit,

the colonel's hit! Bring up a medic, bring up a medic!"
Horst Faas runs up as Eyster's eyes open and in a weak
voice he mutters, "Horst, don't get hit, don't get hit,"
and lapses into unconsciousness.

I am filming the scene with an 8 mm camera. Horst
and I search for the tunnel that we assume the sniper
popped out of. We don't find it.

My story of the Black Lions, filed the following
morning, begins: "It was a long bloody mile we walked
Wednesday. At times it was a Dante's inferno of fire
and brimstone. Powerful riot gas drifted through the
trees, burning where it touched a man's sweating skin.
Wounded American soldiers writhed on the ground,
looking monstrous in their black, grotesque gas masks.
It was a walk where death lurked in the trees where
the enemy snipers hid, and under the ground where
their mines lay."

I don't name Eyster in this story out of concern for
his family. We visit him at a base hospital where he
lies in a barren, uncooled room under a mosquito net.
He is ashen faced and in pain, his neck and chest heavily bandaged, his left arm in a sling. Horst has printed
a few pictures of the previous day's action to show
him, and he gazes with pleasure at them, whispering,
"I had a lucky escape. I nearly didn't make it."

The 3rd Brigade commander phones our bureau
the next afternoon saying Eyster has died overnight.
He invites us to attend the memorial service planned

for the following day at the base. We can't make it. We are already on our way to rejoin the Black Lions because my story has received considerable newspaper play in the United States and editors want more.

Three days later, I write Eyster's obituary. It begins: "He was the son of a general, a West Pointer, and a battalion commander. But Lieutenant Colonel George Eyster was to die like a rifleman. It may have been the colonel's leaves on his shoulder, or the map he held in his hand, or just a wayward chance that the sniper chose Eyster from the five of us standing on that dusty path." His wife, Harriet, reads my story in an Orlando newspaper and writes me, "You gave his children a legacy that no one else could have and his heroism will live for them and be an inspiration to them forever."

The launching of America's conventional war against North Vietnam's infiltrating combat forces sidelines much of the South Vietnamese army to security duties amongst the general population. American military advisers attached to Vietnamese units watch helplessly as sorely needed equipment and supplies flow instead to the new combat arrivals.

I hear about a Vietnamese paratrooper company under communist siege for several weeks at remote Duc Co firebase near the Cambodian border. An American advisory team is with them. I arrange a ride with the 52nd aviation company, a daredevil American outfit based in Pleiku. One of my pilots wears a wide-brimmed hat and has exotic insignia pinned to his jacket. The other has been in the bar with me the previous night and looks hungover. Once in the air, they are all business, piloting their Huey over and around and sometimes under the tops of ancient giant gnarled trees, soaring over triple-canopy growth, and dropping into grassy clearings. I am dizzy and glad as the sandbagged parapets of Duc Co appear and we land briefly on a red clay tarmac. Wounded Vietnamese are pulled aboard as I slip off into the base and the Huey departs.

Inside I see a giant American in a baggy fatigue uniform and a soft khaki cap who is hauling along a wounded Vietnamese soldier with a bloody compress bandage around his right leg. The man is Army Major Norman Schwarzkopf, out of East Orange, New Jersey. He allows me to stay for three hair-raising days as his team helps the Vietnamese airborne troopers survive the constant shelling and combat assaults of communist troops clearly intent on overrunning the camp. Years later in his autobiography, Schwarzkopf tells a couple of stories about me. One claims that in taking me and others outside one rainy night to guide in a medical evacuation helicopter, he asks us to vigorously shake our flashlights as a signal. I allegedly respond, "Major, I've been shaking for the whole two days I've been here."

In 1991, while I'm covering the first Gulf War from Baghdad for CNN, I hear that Schwarzkopf, now commander of the coalition forces attacking Saddam Hussein, gets so mad at my live coverage that he orders CNN broadcasts turned off at his headquarters in Saudi Arabia. Soon after the war I see him at a gala Washington media dinner. He is a guest of the *U.S. News & World Report* magazine publisher Mortimer Zuckerman, and is imposing in his dress blues, receiving the plaudits of well-wishers. He towers over me as I shake his hand. I mention in jest that I'd heard he was not happy with my Baghdad reporting for CNN, and explain in my defense that I am one of the few reporters at the war's beginning who knows how to pronounce his name. A clever man, Schwarzkopf shoots back, "Yes, but with an Iraqi accent."

7

FIGHTING THE WAR OF WORDS

B Y THE FALL OF 1967, the hope of quick American military success in South Vietnam "has died along with the nearly 13,000 Americans soldiers already killed." The observation is from an AP analysis I write about the growing stalemate on the battlefield. It can be broken, I argue, only by bringing in more American troops or by revitalizing the dispirited South Vietnamese army. The 400,000 American soldiers already in combat "could be tied down for a decade just holding the lid on communist forces now active all over the country."

The Associated Press looks to me, by now its longest-serving reporter in Vietnam, to write such assessments of the war. The American military high command often disagrees with them, as it does in this case. Not for the first time, I'm called in by Barry Zorthian, the normally affable former U.S. Marine colonel sent to Saigon in 1965 by President Johnson to manage press relations. He says his superiors in Washington are not happy with my latest story. "Damn it, Peter," Zorthian says, thumping his fist on his desk. "You write these analyses without including our side of the story. That's unfair."

I remind him that his side of the story is given every afternoon in the official Saigon press briefings, regularly attended by other AP staffers, and is sometimes useful but more often not, justifying the sobriquet given by the attendees, "The Five O'clock Follies." And there are the well-covered press conferences hosted by Defense Department, State Department and White House officials in Washington, invariably optimistic about Vietnam. I tell Zorthian my stories are fed into the mix along with all the others, and it's just too bad he's held accountable for the most critical of them. "Well, we don't like what you do," he says.

In April 1966, I have a run-in with Zorthian over what I see as unnecessary roughness by an American military policeman during a Buddhist protest demonstration in Saigon directed against the policies of Prime Minister Nguyen Cao Ky. Stones are flying and voices raised as the protesters square off against Saigon police near an important pagoda. A nervous American MP emerges from the ranks and demands that I and several other western reporters leave the scene. I assert that he doesn't have authority over us, a view backed up by my colleagues including Bob Schieffer, at that time reporting for the *Fort Worth Star-Telegram*.

The MP draws his .45, waves it around, and then points it directly at me as I continue to protest his commands. The tension is worsened by photographer Eddie Adams, an AP colleague sometimes prone to mischief, who starts calling out loudly, "Shoot him. Shoot him. It'll make a better picture." The MP is looking increasingly rattled. He backs off and we continue covering the story.

Eddie got a dramatic picture of the MP in action against us. The next morning, I go to Zorthian's office to complain. He says he's already heard from the State Department and that Secretary Dean Rusk saw the picture in *The Washington Post* and ordered that such things not happen again. Zorthian says his office is considering laying charges against me, anyway.

"What's the charge?" I ask in surprise.

His lips curl. "Assault against a peace officer with a deadly weapon."

"What deadly weapon?" I demand.

He responds with bemusement, "A pen and pencil."

My news coverage of the war depends not on the usual press briefings and insider background sessions with top officials. I rely on the generosity and the collaboration of Americans in the field who have read my stories over the years and trust me. I spend much of my time with combat units, chronicling the endeavors of the officers and ordinary soldiers sent to do battle in an environment uniquely hostile to the American military experience, and against an implacable, always threatening enemy.

I also visit civilian officials in the beleaguered provincial towns where they direct American aid programs and have valuable insights into the local people. The best is John Paul Vann, the gutsy former lieutenant colonel I first met in 1962 when he was a military adviser in the Mekong Delta. He was let go by the Defense Department, partly for his critical outbursts to me and other reporters over South Vietnamese military incompetence in the battle of Ap Bac in January 1963, the first major action of the war. Before he left the Army, though, he submitted a blistering critique of the Pentagon's assistance program, calling its claims of success "a bright shining lie." The phrase became the title of Neil Sheehan's Pulitzer Prize-winning biography of Vann, published in 1988.

When Vann returns to Vietnam early in 1965 as the senior civilian adviser in Hau Nghia province, I get in touch and he offers to drive me around his domain. Positioned to the west of Saigon, his province is one of the most insecure places in the region. Vann runs a pacification program that tries to unite all government security efforts. He picks me up in his jeep at a small Italian-style eatery near our office run by a young Vietnamese woman who affectionately bids him farewell. Vann is bursting with energy, his narrow face burned by the sun, his hair crew cut, his accent decidedly Texan.

Vann says he is happy to be back even as a civilian, and we clear Saigon's suburbs and head into what American military personnel are beginning to call "the boonies." I see a few old French concrete outposts along the highway, manned by local militiamen who, Vann says, rarely go outside because communist guerrillas are everywhere. We turn into a narrow roadway and pass abandoned paddy fields and flattened farmhouses. Vann reaches into the glove compartment and hands me three or four M26 fragmentation hand grenades. I hold them carefully in my lap. "If we hit a roadblock that I don't recognize, throw a hand grenade or pass one to me and I'll do it," he says breezily. "I'm the big man around here."

We arrive at his headquarters, a decrepit former post office in a desolate town that was vacated for a year or so before the government set up authority again. Vann is a great source for a reporter to have. He believes strongly in the mission to maintain an independent South Vietnam, but he disagrees with the massive military buildup and the use of overwhelming firepower to win the war. He's an expert in military tactics and also tuned in to the intricacies of Vietnamese politics. He works tirelessly to turn American attention toward rebuilding the South Vietnamese military and government rather than continuing all-out war. He believes in the tired phrase "winning the hearts and minds of the people," and begins attracting converts to his views. One of them is Daniel Ellsberg, the former Robert McNamara whiz kid who becomes his friend. They plot to try to persuade the secretary of defense to change destructive military policies. Within a year, Vann is chief of the pacification effort in 12 provinces. He's willing to brief me anytime I'm interested. There is a condition. "Don't ever quote me," he says. "Remember what happened the last time."

I never know in advance what will trigger an irate pushback from the military. I write an unflattering assessment of General Westmoreland for the papers of Jan. 27, pointing out that in the three years he has been in Vietnam the war has changed dramatically, that it is 58 times more costly per day, and that American casualties have increased fiftyfold. I quote critics who complain the four-star general has displayed a ruthless ambition, shoring up his base of power by calling for more and more troop deployments when his job had originally been to build up Vietnamese capability to fight their own war. There is no pushback. Then comes the tennis story.

A visiting AP staffer, Kelly Smith, on a break from her coverage of the White House, is offered a "Day with Westmoreland" story by the general's PR people.

Our charming visitor makes the most of it, a break-fast-to-dinner marathon with the trusting general. Some editor in New York suggests we compare the general's day to a typical American combat soldier's experience. On the morning that Kelly is watching Westmoreland shave in the bathroom of his comfortable downtown Saigon home, I am awakening in the midst of an unshaven grunt company from the U.S. 25th Division in the boonies west of Saigon. By evening, after a day of sniper fire has wounded several soldiers, I close my notebook, climb on a medical evacuation helicopter and head home.

Kelly and I compare notes and sit down to write a long feature for Sunday newspapers. Our narrative includes the information that as helicopters are preparing to ferry out wounded from my unit in my day, in Kelly's day Westmoreland is settling into his late-morning workout with his tennis pro at the Cercle Sportif, the former French country club in Saigon. The Saigon high command gets its hands on an advance copy of our story and demands a revision, insisting that the general's tennis game is no one's business but his own. We leave it to AP editors to decide. The tennis stays put.

Two weeks later, I'm waiting with other reporters at an official welcoming ceremony at the U.S. 9th Infantry Division base at My Tho for visiting Vice President Hubert Humphrey. Westmoreland is standing in front of me. He turns, scowling. "Well, you'll be happy to know that I've resigned my membership of the Cercle Sportif," he says. I express surprise and mention that just the previous week, at my wife Nina's suggestion, I'd joined the club so that my young son can go swimming. "Well," the general grunted, "maybe they gave you my membership."

Westmoreland travels to Washington in November at the request of President Johnson, who is eager to quiet public anxieties about his Vietnam policies. In interviews and press conferences, the general expresses confidence that the war will soon be concluded, that he sees "the light at the end of the tunnel." Even as he reassures officials in Washington that all is well and that the communist forces are on the run, North Vietnamese military planners are launching the first of a series of major assaults that within three months will test the resolve of the United States to the breaking point, bring down a president and place the future of South Vietnam in grave doubt.

The enemy picks the time and place for the first battles, the remote valley of Dak To, tucked between two mountain massifs near the Cambodia-Laos border. I fly in an Air Force transport plane packed with combat reinforcements to Pleiku, and hitch an onward ride in an army helicopter to Dak To, landing near a press camp prepared by the 1st Cavalry Division. I throw my pack into a large tent lined with

canvas bunks and woolen blankets. The outdoor priv-
ies are starting to smell. I join an AP reporting team
already assembled there. It is mid-November. By this
time, American spokesmen are estimating that 12,000
communist troops have been steadily digging bunkers
and protective tunnels in the surrounding mountains,
the largest enemy concentration in the whole war so
far. I watch with awe as the skyline erupts all around
me with fiery red explosions and purple, yellow and
white smoke from artillery barrages and airstrikes.
America is throwing everything at the mountains.
Some colleagues are reporting that the communists
have walked into a trap and will be pulverized by
American firepower. Maybe it's the other way around,
in the view of a few.

This time I'm not interested in the big picture
because we learn there is concern about the fate of
three paratrooper companies from the 2nd Battalion
of the 173rd Airborne Brigade. We're told they're out-
flanked to the west and the east near the crest of Hill
875, a pointed knob of triple-canopy jungle and scrub
poking up from the valley floor. The brigade is immediately sending a relief mission of three paratrooper
companies from the 4th Battalion. They'll be moving on foot through the jungle, and three journalists
from our number are invited to go. We are warned it is
extremely dangerous, much of the trip will be at night,
and that we will be offered no special consideration.

I pull rank by asserting that I'm the senior reporter there, and working for the world's biggest news organization. I get to go.

The next 36 hours are the most dangerous in my life. There are 500 of us in the relief party, at the beginning slogging up a ridgeline overgrown with thick bamboo trees and low underbrush. By afternoon the landscape changes into high forest with towering teak and mahogany trees. At dusk, we are still two miles from ascending Hill 875. As darkness falls we move single file, holding hands along a narrow trail to avoid getting lost. The enemy knows we are coming, and hidden gunners occasionally open up with anti-tank guns. The shells tear over our heads and explode in the trees around us with balls of fire. We scatter until it's over, and then move on.

By midevening we are on the slopes of Hill 875 and use hanging vines to help pull ourselves up. In the moonlight we see shapes of dead bodies, and a soldier near me yells out, "We've killed a lot of gooks," until we approach closer and see they are the bodies of dead Americans wearing only their skivvies— their uniforms, boots and weapons carried off by the enemy. Near the crest we come upon the main group, and gasp at what we find. Mounds of dead paratroops lie spread-eagled where they have fallen. Behind pitiful barricades of tree branches hide the wounded.

I find an open patch of dirt and borrow a soldier's entrenching tool and start digging a shallow foxhole to spend the night. But the metal strikes at human flesh, a body buried there by a bomb explosion earlier in the day. I recoil in horror and step back on something soft and find it is a detached arm from another corpse. I look about me in the moonlight and feel ill. I have been proud of a certain professional detachment, but now I feel ashamed of my neutrality, useless with my notebooks and cameras and water bottles. I don't even carry a gun, so I am just one more liability for the surviving defenders.

But I can write their story. Following a somber day of interviews and self-reflection, I leave on a medical evacuation helicopter. At the Dak To airstrip I sleep under the wing of a transport plane scheduled to leave at dawn for the coastal base of Qui Nhon. When we land I run to the communication shack and plead with a technician to help me. On the phone, he gets my pal Ed White, who is manning the day desk in Saigon. I type furiously, then hand the technician the first long paragraph:

> War painted the living and the dead the same gray color on Hill 875. The only way to tell who was alive and who was dead amongst the exhausted men was to watch when the enemy mortars came crashing in. The living rushed unashamedly to the tiny bunkers dug into the red clay of the hilltop. The wounded squirmed toward

the shelter of trees that had been blasted to the ground. Only the dead didn't move, propped up in the bunkers where they had died in direct mortar hits, or face down in the dust where they had fallen to bullets.

Within an hour Ed White has the whole story. He quickly sends it on its way via telex to AP New York, and thence to America's newspapers, whose editors will decide if the fate of those on Hill 875 merits the attention of an anxious country. I'm sure of one thing: Barry Zorthian's superiors in Washington won't be pleased.

Ten weeks later, firecrackers pop and paper dragons dance from their strings. The year of the dragon is here. It is Tet 1968, the Vietnamese New Year, a time to celebrate for the war-weary people of Saigon, me and my family among them. Something is wrong, though, as I try to sleep. The fireworks' crack seems much more intense than usual, more like the snap of passing bullets. Passing bullets? I spring wide-awake at a sound I do recognize, that of a 50-caliber machine gun firing nervous bursts.

I open my balcony door overlooking Rue Pasteur in the heart of Saigon. I see it's a nervous sentry at the entrance to the old Gia Long Palace across the street. Then the phone rings. It's Ed White. "Hey man, they're here, the communists, all over the city. Get your butt down to the bureau." I push my wife and two children into our thick-walled bathroom and toss in a mattress for extra protection.

I walk quickly to our bureau three blocks away and try not to appear excited. No point in being mistaken for an enemy combatant. I hear heavy gunfire now, from the presidential palace four blocks to the east, from the U.S. Embassy a similar distance to the northeast. I soon learn that the communist guerrillas are emerging from their exile in the swamps and jungles to invade South Vietnam's cities and towns in an attempt to force America to change its war policies. Forty targets of significance are hit hard across the country.

Complete surprise, that's what John Paul Vann tells me at his Bien Hoa headquarters later in the day. Only once before in Vietnam's history of frequent violent conflict has the sanctity of Tet been so blatantly violated. In the late 18th century, General Nguyen Hue stole upon a Chinese garrison holding Hanoi that was lulled into believing that Tet meant truce. The unsuspecting Chinese were annihilated.

I fly with a few news colleagues on a government-organized trip to the provincial capital of Ben Tre in the central Mekong Delta, which we hear was the subject of a repulsed communist attack. I had been there before and while the others are loading into a bus for a visit to downtown, I hitch a ride with Major Chester L. Brown, an Air Force officer who had flown me around in his tiny L-19 spotter plane on my previous visit. He warns I will be shocked at what I see, that Ben Tre is in ruins, and that many people have died.

"It is always a pity about the civilians," he says. "In the mass confusion of this kind of thing, the people don't know where the lines are, they don't know where to hide, and some of the weapons we were using were area weapons instead of against specific targets, and that way people get hurt."

He drops me off at the American military advisory compound; it and the governor's headquarters look like the only places undamaged. I bring up Major Brown's remarks with an Army major I had met before. He thinks about it for a minute and mentions that when the town seemed about to be overrun by communist attackers, he ordered in the heavy firepower. "We had to destroy the town in order to save it," he says.

By the time the bloody battles of Tet 1968 are over, the authorities report that 3,000 South Vietnamese and American soldiers have been killed, along with 8,000 civilians. Some 40,000 communist soldiers are claimed killed, if true virtually wiping out the local communist guerrilla organizations. Westmoreland claims a major victory, maybe true enough if Vietnam's war is based solely on a high attrition rate, the ratio of our dead to theirs. But the war has become a political struggle, and much of the American public turns against it for two main reasons, the steady diet of optimism fed to it by the Johnson administration that is so dramatically challenged by the Tet attacks, and Westmoreland's request for another 206,000 American soldiers even as he declares a mighty victory.

President Johnson has his back to the wall. He is still unforgiving of critical news stories and distressing photographs that in previous wars would have been stopped by the censorship he was politically afraid of implementing in this war. He calls the AP personnel chief, Keith Fuller, to the White House. Fellow Texans, they chat over a lunch of hamburgers in the Oval Office. The president tells Fuller he decided to pull his information specialist Barry Zorthian out of Saigon, "because he has been there too long." Then, as Fuller later tells me, Johnson asks, "Now hasn't that Australian Pete Arnett been there too long, too?"

The president decides in March 1968 that he's through with the Vietnam War. His popularity is crashing. There are the strong showings by competing Democratic politicians in the presidential primaries. He stuns the nation by announcing he won't run for a second term, and calls for negotiations with the North Vietnamese.

Westmoreland will soon leave, a rotation determined months before but interpreted by many as a rebuke for the Tet Offensive surprise. He becomes chief of staff of the army, a prestigious appointment, but he finds it difficult to shake off the growing controversies over the war. After he retires, in 1973, he agrees to let me accompany him and his son, Rip, for a few days for a story as they drive around South Carolina, seeking votes for his candidacy in the Republican primary contest for the governorship. I note that Westmoreland is a man who, in his bemedaled army dress uniform and manly bearing, has become as familiar to Americans as any other person, but in his civilian clothes, pushing open a door at McDonald's looking for votes, he is not recognized. Westmoreland is good-humored about it all, and after he loses sends me a note of thanks for my tongue-in-cheek story about his campaign.

The general also agrees to a two-day television interview I conduct with him for a Canadian documentary on Vietnam, and I see him at a few of the military-media conferences on war reporting being held around the country at that time. I have a final meeting, a year or so before his death in 2005, when I'm in Charleston, South Carolina, speaking at a charity event organized by an acquaintance, John Winship. He suggests I visit his friend, and I agree. We drive to Westmoreland's home at an upscale retirement community in a suburban neighborhood. We're met at the door by his wife, Kitsy, and she chats for a moment about a meeting we had in Saigon early in the war. Her husband sits in the bright sunlight of a room with a wall full of windows, white haired now and frail looking. He nods to me, squinting a little, seeing a familiar face from a long-ago war that is fading slowly from memory. I thank him for phoning his old friend Tom Johnson, the president of CNN, in 1991, praising my live coverage of the Gulf War from Baghdad, even though he'd also expressed reservations about what I'd done in Saigon.

"Peter," he says, "I think your reporting from Vietnam was OK. But I'll never forgive you for that tennis story."

8

NIXON'S BIGGER PICTURE

R ICHARD NIXON is visiting Saigon in mid-April 1967 to burnish his foreign policy credentials as he considers a run for the presidency the following year, and I'm assigned to spend a day with the former vice president. He is getting the usual VIP treatment from the American Embassy and the Vietnamese, meeting with Prime Minister Nguyen Cao Ky before arriving at the airport where I wait with a few other reporters to accompany him on a helicopter trip to the countryside. He is in shirtsleeves and sweating in the stifling heat.

I've heard that Nixon dislikes the press. His bitter outcry to reporters after losing the California governor's race in 1962, that "you won't have Nixon to kick around anymore," resonates gleefully in combative newsrooms around the country. But he is effusively friendly here. He shakes my hand. He nods over to where some uniformed local girls are bringing cold drinks. "Good-looking, hmm," he says, grinning. He is equally amiable to the American soldiers and civilian officials he meets in Mekong Delta encampments during the day, listening thoughtfully to the briefings. There's not much news, though. Nixon's a well-known hawk on the war and repeats his support of it. He continues his forceful criticism of the anti-war protests growing in intensity back home, saying they weaken the soldiers' fighting spirit. He leaves early the following morning.

Nixon takes office as the 37th president of the United States in January 1969. He quickly assures a war-weary public he won't seek military victory in Vietnam and will soon start bringing the troops home. But his off-the-cuff remarks to our handful of reporters at the Saigon airport 21 months earlier are prophetic. As president, Nixon seems unmoved by anti-war protest, and his increasingly bellicose military undertakings while in office do not cool off public dissent but trigger more. And he is unhurried in winding down the U.S. role in the war. It will be a long four years later, with the combat deaths of an additional 20,000 Americans, before the last soldiers come home.

Veterans of the embattled administration of the previous president, Lyndon Johnson, blame Nixon for unnecessarily delaying the war's end. "The American people at the grass roots had come to the conclusion that we should abandon the effort," says Johnson's secretary of state, Dean Rusk, one of several former officials I interview for a television documentary after the war.

Rusk says he is surprised that Nixon takes so long to bring about a "particular result" rather than to simply extract American forces, greatly reducing the conflict. "There was no suggestion of defeat in an American withdrawal," Rusk adds. "We had left behind for the Nixon administration a military position which the North Vietnamese could not have overrun." The particular result he mentioned was the ceasefire agreement signed in Paris by Henry Kissinger and a North Vietnamese official, Le Duc Tho, effective Jan. 28, 1973.

But Nixon's chief of staff, H.R. Haldeman, also interviewed for my television project, says that Nixon had no intention of quickly pulling out of Vietnam. Unlike Johnson, who was primarily interested in domestic affairs, Nixon is fixated on foreign policy. "Vietnam was an expedient, a kind of stage where America's bona fides, our intentions, our motives, were being acted out," Haldeman says. Nixon aimed to defuse the forces of world communism by exploiting the rivalry between China and the Soviet Union and improving America's relations with both of them, thereby achieving détente and limitation of arms. "Nixon believed America had to negotiate from strength, to prove its willingness to fight. Vietnam became that place," Haldeman says.

Nixon weaves his grand foreign policy designs behind White House doors, aided and encouraged by Kissinger, a Harvard-educated political scientist known as a brilliant and pragmatic strategist. They set in motion a "Vietnamization" plan to soften the blow of the American withdrawal. It is ambitious, calling for the gradual rearming and retraining of the whole South Vietnamese military establishment as a permanent buffer against the communists.

Nixon's decision to delay withdrawing troops to achieve his military and political goals means that numbers are reduced by only 60,000 at the end of his first year in office. Nearly 500,000 remain, most of them young draftees. Families at home are impatient for their return. The burden facing U.S. military authorities is to extract under fire a demoralized fighting force increasingly prone to behavior that strains military discipline and the code of conduct.

On my trips to the battlefield I find that American soldiers are aware that they are fighting a holding action until the Vietnamese are ready to shoulder their own burden. For many, there is less personal incentive to win than there used to be, but the dangers are just as real. The soldiers see the final phase as uncertain. Under Nixon, every year the combat keeps escalating: In 1969 the secret bombing of Cambodia, in 1970 the invasion of Cambodia, in 1971 the invasion of Laos, in 1972 a new major offensive by North Vietnam.

Photographer Horst Faas and I stumble on a story late in August 1969 that some see as a harbinger of things to come. We are with troops of the Americal Infantry Division searching for the wreckage of an observation helicopter shot down a few days earlier. The AP photographer Ollie Noonan was believed aboard. I am with the commander of the 196th Light Infantry Brigade, Lieutenant Colonel Robert C. Bacon, at his field bivouac in the northern coastal mountains near the crash scene when I hear these words over a crackling field telephone: "I'm sorry, sir, but my men refuse to go. We cannot move out." They are spoken by Lieutenant Eugene Shurtz Jr., the commander of the battalion's A Company. The unit has been ordered at dawn to move once more down the jungled rocky slope of Nui Lon Mountain into a deadly labyrinth of North Vietnamese bunkers and trench lines.

A Company is one of three units involved in the assault. Colonel Bacon pales as Shurtz matter-offactly tells him that the soldiers of A Company will not follow orders. "Repeat that, please," the colonel asks without raising his voice. "Have you told them what it means to disobey orders under fire?"

"I think they understand," the lieutenant replies, "but some of them simply have had enough. They are broken. There are boys here who have only 90 days left in Vietnam. They want to go home in one piece. The situation is psychic here."

"Are you talking about enlisted men or are NCOs involved," the colonel asks.

"That's the difficulty here. We've got a leadership problem," replies the company commander. "Most of our squad and platoon leaders have been killed or wounded." I learn that at one point in the fight A Company was down to 60 men, half its assigned combat strength.

Colonel Bacon quietly tells his company commander, "Go talk to them again and tell them that to the best of our knowledge the bunkers are now empty. The enemy has withdrawn. The mission of A Company today is to recover the dead. They have no reason to be afraid. Please take a hand count of how many really do not want to go."

Lieutenant Shurtz comes back a few minutes later, saying, "They won't go, Colonel. And I did not ask for the hand count because I'm afraid they will all stick together even though some might prefer to go."

By late afternoon, with some coaxing from the most experienced men in the battalion who fly to A Company's location and make personal appeals, A Company does move. They are led by a seasoned veteran, Sergeant Okey Blankenship of Panther, West Virginia, who, quick tempered and argumentative, talks the reluctant soldiers into rejoining the war.

The A Company story gets a lot of attention from editors and readers who have stopped thinking much about the soldiers still left in Vietnam. There is much editorial comment. The *Washington Star* newspaper in an editorial tends to dismiss the implications. "There have been suggestions from some quarters that Alpha company's brief 'mutiny' may presage a revolt among young draftees serving in Vietnam who are unwilling to die in an admittedly unwinnable war in which many Americans feel this country never had any business. There is not a scintilla of evidence to support this, and those who suggest it display little knowledge of what soldiering is all about. There have been similar incidents in every conflict since the Punic wars."

James Reston of *The New York Times* is more concerned, writing, "This is something that President Nixon needs to be worried about as he plans his Vietnam policy. He has been worried about the revolt of the voters against the war and even a revolt of the generals if he humiliates them by pulling out too fast. But now he must also consider the possibility of a revolt of the men if he risks their lives in a war he has decided to bring to a close."

In late March 1972, the North Vietnamese launch a conventional invasion against the south. The objective, it is later learned, is not to win the war but to gain as much territory and to destroy as many units of the South Vietnamese army as possible. In this Easter Offensive they gain substantial territory and influence the peace negotiations coming to a head in Paris.

I have a last visit with John Paul Vann during the offensive. He is now the senior American official in the Central Highlands, a strategic region the Saigon government must hold to have any hope of enduring as a legitimate state. I hear some reporters dismiss Vann as "the last American hawk in the war." He tells me he gets upset by what he describes as the "triviality" of the questions thrown at him at press conferences. I advise him that he can't win a war with the media.

I notice Vann is more animated than usual. He's just returned to Pleiku from three days in the besieged provincial capital of Kontum. To blunt the frequent enemy attacks, he says he has orchestrated around-the-clock U.S. Air Force B-52 bomber strikes. It is probably one of the most enormous concentrations of firepower used in the war. Vann insists that it's working. He praises the Vietnamese general in command in Kontum, Ly Tong Ba, whom I had heard Vann scolding 10 years earlier at the disastrous battle of Ap Bac for not being sufficiently aggressive with his armored patrol. "You should see him now," he says proudly.

Vann says he's traveling down to the coastal city of Qui Nhon and offers me a ride. He directs the helicopter pilot to fly over Mang Yang, a twisting, jungled, narrow pass that opens the highlands to the South China Sea. In an infamous battle during the French war, an elite mobile infantry unit was ambushed there and destroyed by the communists. Vann shouts at me over the helicopter clatter, "They say the French dead were buried right here, standing up and facing France. If I'm to die, that's what I want, standing upright here and facing east to Texas."

Vann did die here a few weeks later, on Jun. 9, 1972. His helicopter crashed on a night flight to Kontum with the loss of everyone on board. Vann was a maverick, an anti-establishment outsider who forced his way inside, one of the last Americans who believed in victory in Vietnam, and died trying to achieve it. Vann received a hero's funeral in Washington, D.C., with some in attendance who had derided his earlier efforts in Vietnam and who now came to mourn. It was great for his family. My thought was that if Vann had anything to say about it, he would have preferred being buried standing up in his beloved Vietnam, and facing east across the great Pacific Ocean to Texas.

In mid-August of 1972, I'm invited to visit the other side, a rare trip to Hanoi, the North Vietnamese capital, to cover the journey of a prominent group of peace advocates. They've been promised the opportunity to bring back home three captured Navy pilots to be released from the "Hanoi Hilton" prison on the occasion of their visit. The mother of one prisoner and the wife of another will go. I want to go. I know it's a propaganda ploy by the communists to win sympathy for their side as the peace talks drag on in Paris. But

I figure that I can outwit them enough to give credibility to my coverage. AP president Wes Gallagher is concerned about my participation because both Jane Fonda and Anthony Lewis of *The New York Times* have incurred storms of criticism for their visits to North Vietnam earlier in the year. He looks at me under furrowed brows. "Peter, it's your reputation and mine on the line this time."

Two of the travelers are national figures. One is David Dellinger, a shaggy-haired, fervid peace activist, known as one of the Chicago Seven anti-war protesters at the 1968 Democratic National Convention in Chicago. He turns out to be a gentle man with a wry sense of humor. The second is the Reverend William Sloane Coffin, a boisterous former CIA operative who was undercover in a small town for years in the Soviet Union after World War II, later the chaplain at Yale University, and currently a Christian clergyman. A third member is Richard Falk, a professor at Princeton University, author of 20 books on international law. And there's Cora Weiss, a peace activist headquartered in a handsome home in the upscale Riverdale section of the Bronx. She arranges the trip through her Hanoi connections. While I am visiting Cora the phone in her kitchen rings often. She tells me she is bugged by the FBI and other government agencies because of her anti-war activities. In Martha's Vineyard where she says she had a home, "the tap was so loud the phone spluttered and jumped on the hook all night, and imagine that when you're lying in bed with your husband." She protests to a State Department security officer, who tells her, "That's not my bug, mine's not so powerful. That's Laird's." Melvin Laird is secretary of defense.

We arrive in Hanoi from Vientiane, Laos, on a regular flight of the International Control Commission, a body that loosely supervises previous political agreements between the two Vietnams. I am assigned a young woman named Lien as an escort and I walk through nearly empty, noiseless streets, the silence sometimes broken by the sharp tinkle of a bicycle bell. I pass the dust-covered old French colonial buildings, and in the more densely populated areas the paint is peeling off the walls of the little shops and the timbers are rotting. The people are dressed mostly in somber garments, usually black trousers and white or gray shirts and blouses. I think of Saigon, where I had been just the week before, its economy swelled by American dollars, with its atmosphere of a boom town, sidewalks crowded with soldiers but also beautiful young women, its highways congested with flashy motorcycles, sporty cars and jeeps.

In Saigon, the action seems far away, the crackle of distant gunfire sometimes the only indication there is a war on. In Hanoi, fear floats in on the dust. I hear the squawk of loudspeakers. My escort translates,

"American planes 70 kilometers out," the first warning to the population of approaching airstrikes. Soon after, the announcement, "American planes 50 kilometers out." The sirens start to wail when the planes are within 40 kilometers. People search out the single-berth bunkers built like cisterns, with steel lids, along every street. Wardens alert people in houses to move into roomier shelters. Then a quiet settles over the city as people wait to see how close the bombers come. The siren wails the all-clear. The planes are active elsewhere in the country this day.

The three U.S. pilots are released to our care: Navy Lieutenants Mark Gartley and Norris Charles, and Air Force Major Edward Elias. Elias bunks with me at our hotel, and at first he is disconcerted to discover I'm a reporter, but then he settles down. He's had worse conditions at the Hanoi Hilton prison. One day we all travel to the countryside, where the pilots observe that years of American bombing have failed to achieve significant results. We repeatedly encounter vehicle convoys, rows of stacked ammunition along the roadsides and piles of gasoline drums. We pass scores of transportation trucks casually parked under trees, and to me they look vulnerable to airstrikes. Norris Charles tells me, "We could never see those things from the air, and the moment someone comes down for a better look, blam, blam, blam."

The peace advocate group has good connections in Hanoi. We are invited to visit with Prime Minister Pham Van Dong at his palatial government residence near Ho Chi Minh's tomb. He's a handsome, silver-haired figure, and friendly, giving bear hugs to all. At a formal meeting in his office where tea and cookies are served, he reiterates Hanoi's hard line on the war. Afterward, he insists we go walk with him informally on the grounds of his residence. He radiates confidence and determination.

As Vietnamization is speedily upgraded, so do the North Vietnamese respond with a military upgrading of their own. The legendary Ho Chi Minh Trail infiltration gateway stretching across mountainous border regions is engineered into a two-lane highway, allowing military supply trucks just a day or so to make the journey from north to south; a few years earlier, it could take foot soldiers dragging bicycles weighed down with ammunition 60 days to travel over the then primitive path.

Gearing up to fight a stronger Vietnamese army supported for the time being by the American troops and their firepower still in-country, the communists do not match the eventual American troop withdrawal with one of their own. Hanoi's forces remain in the south in the scores of thousands, the ceasefire agreement allowing them to do so. Nixon's strategy has paved the way for his historic opening to China in 1972, and détente with Russia. But with America increasingly absent from the battlefield, it leaves the South Vietnamese with an almost overwhelming burden of survival.

Arnett and an American military photographer assist a wounded South Vietnamese soldier to an ambulance south of Hue, circa 1969.
(Peter Arnett Collection)

South Vietnamese military police with fixed bayonets escort AP reporter Peter Arnett, center, and cameraman Larry Bedford away from the Chu Van An high school in Saigon, September 1963, where Vietnamese troops arrested scores of high school boys. (AP Photo)

Arnett is held at gunpoint by U.S. military policeman during Buddhist crisis in Saigon, circa 1966; at left is CBS's Bob Schieffer, then a reporter for the *Dallas Morning News*. (Peter Arnett Collection)

Arnett on patrol with South Vietnamese paratroopers in the province of Binh Dinh, Vietnam, 1965. (AP Photo)

The body of a slain comrade is carried to an evacuation helicopter by soldiers of the U.S. 1st Cavalry Division in the Ia Drang Valley early in the week of Nov. 15, 1965. (AP Photo/Peter Arnett)

Arnett, third from left, poses with members of President Carter's Commission to Hanoi in March 1977. The Commission was there to investigate missing American soldiers and seek better relations. (Peter Arnett Collection)

Sitting in a Vietcong tunnel system used during the war, but now turning into a tourist attraction at Cu Chi east of Saigon, 1985. Arnett was visiting Vietnam on the 10th anniversary of the fall of Saigon. (Peter Arnett Collection)

Arnett talks with North Vietnamese Prime Minister Pham Van Dong during visit to Hanoi, August 1972. (Peter Arnett Collection)

Reunion of Pulitzer Prize winners from AP in New York on May 10, 1966. Fifth from left is Peter Arnett. (AP Photo)

Arnett in Saigon in 1970 with wife, Nina, daughter, Elsa, and son, Andrew. (Peter Arnett Collection)

9

FALSE PEACE / FALSE HOPES

I N 1973, the AP sends me back to Saigon from New York, where I have moved with my family after years of covering the war. I'm to write about how South Vietnam can survive alone without American troops and with cuts in Congressional funding. The attention of the American public and the government is centered on the Watergate scandal swamping President Nixon. Internationally, the Middle East shuttle diplomacy of Henry Kissinger is in the news. The Vietnam story, our new foreign editor, Nate Polowetzky, tells me, has moved to the back pages of America's newspapers, "amidst the truss ads," and he hopes I can stir up some editorial interest.

I take my wife, Nina, and our children, Elsa and Andrew, with me, to where they were born and where their relatives live in the shadow of an uncertain future. Saigon itself seems unwilling to face up to the consequences of a decade of inconclusive war and an ambivalent peace agreement. The morning traffic quietens for early afternoon siesta time, speeding up in the evening when the restaurants and nightclubs flourish. I get a first impression that an Indian summer has arrived in South Vietnam, a false peace like the one I read about in the 1930s in Europe that preceded World War II.

Deciding to take advantage of it, I rent a serviceable Chevy van and driver, borrow an interpreter from the AP bureau and head up national Route 1 as far as I can go. I take my 9-year-old son, Andrew along, so he can see where his dad spent much of the previous 10 years covering the war. Over the next two weeks, I interview Vietnamese provincial government officials, visit regional military headquarters and combat bases, and talk with local people. Andrew enjoys playing in the roadside dumpsites among the abandoned battle tanks and artillery pieces, and he shoots down imaginary enemy planes from rusting anti-aircraft guns.

We reach the old imperial capital of Hue, where white-flannelled tennis players are competing in the Northern Provincial Invitation Meet at the local Cercle Sportif club. Just 40 miles north up Route 1, opposite the ruins of Quang Tri city on the banks of the Thach Han River, I see a tent city, a forward command post of the enemy, flying clusters of Communist flags.

After traveling to other parts of the country, I begin to see that the communists are establishing a "third Vietnam" of interconnecting highways and embryonic towns in the third of the country that fell to them in North Vietnam's Easter Offensive the previous year. It stretches 600 miles inside South Vietnam, from the 17th parallel border in the north to the Seven Mountains near the Gulf of Thailand to the south. The sites of battles I had covered in the Central Highlands and the northern border during the war are now in the enemy's hands: Khe Sanh, the Ia Drang Valley, Dak To, firebases Duc Co and Kate, the Rockpile, and many others.

My analyses appear in the Asian editions of the *Stars and Stripes* military newspaper still available in Saigon, and displease Vietnamese officials including the information minister, Hoang Duc Nha, who calls me to his office for a dressing-down. Nha takes exception to a quote in my stories from Colonel Vo Toan, a regimental commander in the 1st Infantry Division at Hue. The quote: "If a major communist offensive begins I'll be pushed away from the western defenses of Hue and into the city within 48 hours if the U.S. doesn't send in B-52s, and I want everything else, F-4s, A-1s, the whole lot." He is referring to the most effective ground support aircraft in America's arsenal.

Nha is also uncomfortable with my quote from a longtime U.S. Embassy acquaintance in Saigon, Frank Scotton, well known for his insights on the war, who tells me the United States is not trying to win in Vietnam anymore, nor prevent the inevitable communist takeover. "Anti-communist Vietnam today is like ice in a river. You can walk across the ice right now, you can spin stones across it, but the river underneath is flowing swiftly and melting the ice," Scotton says.

Nha scoffs. "You listen to people who don't see the big picture," he tells me. "We are confident we will survive." Not known publicly at the time, and revealed during the South's last desperate days in April 1975, was the reason for the Saigon government's confidence. It arises from South Vietnam's bitter opposition to the Paris peace agreement's permitting North Vietnam to leave many of its combat units in the south. President Nixon, impatient to have President Thieu sign the agreement, applies pressure. Nha recalls in an interview for this book that Nixon writes "many letters" to Thieu, including one that threatens, "If you don't sign it we will go it alone."

Nha tells me after the war, "This was when we became pragmatic. We're not dumb enough to stand in front of a steamroller. If we don't agree, we'll have to get out, and then someone else will become president. But we still love our country, we can still do something. We can ride on the steamroller not under it." The threat is cushioned by Nixon reminding Thieu of the $1 billion shipment of military hardware the he'd rushed to Saigon a month or so earlier. Nixon also makes a commitment to have American military forces re-enter the war if the North Vietnamese launch an overwhelming invasion.

Nha's comments are confirmed in an interview I have with Ambassador Ellsworth Bunker after the war, who tells me, "Thieu received assurances which I gave him personally, written assurances from the president, that in case of a violation of the Paris Agreement by the other side we would come to their [South Vietnam's] assistance. As a result of these commitments, the South Vietnamese signed the Paris Agreement."

By mid-1973 the U.S. Congress is asserting a role in the war. The War Powers Act of 1973 becomes law despite Nixon's veto, the legislation imposing restrictions on the executive branch and requiring consultation with Congress on future war actions.

Congress also orders the bombing of Cambodia to end on Aug. 15. I travel to Phnom Penh from Saigon to cover the story, and drive with colleagues 20 or so miles into the countryside. We walk through tangled underbrush to a grassy patch on the southern bank of the Mekong River, and wait. Early afternoon we hear the planes before we see them, two U.S. Air Force F-4 Phantom jets flying out of a base in Thailand. As they dive toward the village, we see far across the broad river, the sun glinting on silver wings. We see flames and smoke arise from the village, but the aircraft are already climbing and on their way before we hear the bursting bombs. I'd seen a lot of American airstrikes and I would see a lot more in the future. But this is the last I'll see launched in Southeast Asia in the 20th century. In Saigon, Hoang Duc Nha is alarmed by the news. "To us it was a signal. I tell my president, 'Hey, this is the beginning. Put it together with Nixon's Watergate crisis and the unsympathetic view of Congress toward us. We have to be worried.'" Thieu assures him he has confidence in the future.

Nha, who spent much time in the United States in the 1960s, senses America has lost desire to worry about Vietnam. Through 1974, as bloody skirmishes increase in the countryside between the opposing forces, Nha says he counsels his colleagues on the National Security Council to rethink the strategy of trying to hold provinces from the north to the south. Better to consolidate in a more defensible position. They see him as a Cassandra, a persistent bearer of bad news. Thieu moves him out of the government, but remains his friend. Looking back, Nha says, "Our top officials saw America as the big brother riding the B-52s to save us, the little brother."

President Gerald Ford assumes the presidency in August 1974, after the resignation of Nixon. The communists launch an offensive against the important province of Phuoc Long north of Saigon to test America's intentions. By Jan. 7 the provincial capital of Phuoc Binh has fallen after three weeks of fighting, with the South Vietnamese defenders, by accounts, acquitting themselves well. Ford's response, the resumption of reconnaissance flights over the north, prompts President Thieu to complain to friends, "He sends doves, not B-52s."

Ambassador Graham Martin flies back to the United States to try to explain to Congress the gravity of the situation. He runs into another visitor, Tran Van Lam, the president of the South Vietnamese Senate, who is not well received by the Congress. The senator returns to Saigon and tells President Thieu not only was it highly unlikely there would be any supplemental aid, it was unlikely they would receive any aid at all in the next fiscal year, beginning in June.

Graham Martin worries that Thieu's stubborn confidence will crack. "If you try to stiffen someone's back by giving them assurances you yourself do not believe, you are getting nowhere," Martin tells me. He explains to Thieu the deterioration of the climate in the United States, trying to be as realistic as possible. But he sees that the Vietnamese leader still has not lost faith in a last-minute American rescue of South Vietnam with its air force armada.

In an interview in London after the war for a television documentary I was working on, Thieu remembers thinking, "The United States had kept 300,000 troops in Europe for 30 years after the war, had kept 30,000 troops in Korea for 20 years after that war.

And now we had let all American troops withdraw. We just asked for help to fight the war. Instead of maintaining half a million troops in Vietnam it would be 20 times less expensive for the American people. What more could they ask from a small nation?"

10

A "SHATTERING"
FINAL OFFENSIVE

THE RAPIDLY EMERGING communist military threat to the existence of South Vietnam comes cloaked in an air of mystery. The communist side makes a virtue of secrecy, its generals rarely seen in public while they plan the grand designs of war in nondescript buildings in Hanoi, or, when traveling to the southern battlefields, sometimes preferring to be incognito, dressed in commonplace clothing. Within a closed society where the media is just another tool of government, secrets are easily kept and obedience is mandatory.

So it is that the 50-year-old General Van Tien Dung, chief of staff of the North Vietnamese armed forces, clandestinely assembles the largest military armada in his country's long history of warfare. The mission, ordered by the Hanoi Politburo, is to finally liberate the south after a struggle that began in the late 1950s. His planning is helped by the legendary General Vo Nguyen Giap, who orchestrated the successful war against the French, and launched the later war against the Americans.

General Dung is to accompany his troops into the first battle area in the Western Highlands, and he travels by road, his command group code-named A-75. Once in South Vietnam he uses the highway system his forces have covertly constructed in the years since the 1973 Paris Agreements, a new network that replaces the old Ho Chi Minh Trail and is later revealed to have been constructed with 30,000 combat soldiers and "shock youth," including women. One 25-foot-wide paved stretch reaches from the border to Loc Ninh, near Saigon, and is the terminus for 3,000 miles of oil pipelines and a cable-telephone link with Hanoi.

General Dung's first target is Ban Me Thuot in the southern Central Highlands of South Vietnam, a nondescript city with a population of 150,000, a political and economic center and the headquarters of the South's 25th Infantry Division. Saigon intelligence is vaguely aware of communist troop movements in the highlands, but assumes they are directed at the two more important and better defended cities farther to the north, Pleiku and Kontum. The presence of the highest-ranking communist general, if known, would immediately have set alarm bells ringing in Saigon, but Dung's concealment holds, helped by an elaborate subterfuge in Hanoi that has his Volga sedan making trips from his home to military headquarters at 8 a.m. and 2 p.m. each day, and at 5 p.m. soldiers going to the courtyard at his home to play volleyball, a recreation he is known to enjoy.

General Dung provides graphic details of the opening shots of the final communist offensive in a series of articles published in Hanoi the following year. He says he personally commanded the battle from a nearby observation point. At 2 o'clock on the morning of March 10, 1975, Dung's forces assemble under the towering forests of the Cambodian border mountains, move through the tangled undergrowth around primitive villages and abandoned rubber plantations, and head toward Ban Me Thuot. His intelligence has determined that his attacking force has an advantage of 5.5 troops to 1 over the other side.

Dung writes, "Our long-range artillery begins destroying the military targets in the city. No sooner has it opened fire than the lights go out. The airfield is ablaze. From 40 kilometers away our tank units start their engines; modern ferryboats are rapidly assembled to cross rivers, as queues form of waiting armored vehicles and anti-aircraft guns. The mountains and the forests of the Central Highlands are shaken by our firestorm. Basically, the battle was over by 10:30 the next morning."

Shaken also is President Thieu in Saigon. He makes a decision that many see as a major strategic error. He orders that his forces abandon the whole Central Highlands area and regroup along the populated coast. By March 16, thousands of panicked soldiers and their families struggle over a sometimes impassably rough highway to reach the coast. Hundreds die. This "vale of tears" sets the emotional climate for the weeks to follow. General Dung writes that he can't understand that his unexpected blow against Ban Me Thuot has produced "such a shattering impact" on the enemy. But it is a blow that is constantly repeated in the next 50 days, to its victorious conclusion for General Dung in Saigon on April 30.

An enthralled world watches throughout April 1975 as the high drama of South Vietnam's destruction plays out in international newspaper and television reports. Depending on the point of view, what transpires is either the shameful betrayal by a superpower of one of its most vulnerable allies, or the glorious triumph of a long, bloody struggle by communist revolutionaries fighting to secure the independence of their country.

For North Vietnamese Ambassador Ha Van Lau, watching from his post in Havana, Cuba, and hearing cheers in the streets from supporters in this close communist ally, the news is intoxicating. "We are becoming the masters of our own land. Independent.

The most glorious moment in our history," he says in an interview after the war for a television show I am writing.

For Nguyen Ngoc Linh, an old friend of mine, who as a student in New York City in the early 1950s sometimes helped out the monastic Ngo Dinh Diem, who later became the doomed president of South Vietnam, the events are heartbreaking. Linh returned to Saigon to establish a renowned English language school in the 1960s, and worked with the government for a few years before building a successful fishing business. In the closing weeks of the war, unable to get permission from a panicked government for his family to leave, Linh puts his wife and children in the locked-down hatch of one of his fishing boats and has the captain sail through Saigon River security patrols to the open sea and safety in Singapore. "I saw it as the end of my dreams for me and my country," he tells me in an interview for this book in Arlington, Virginia, where he lives with many other educated Vietnamese who made new lives for themselves in America after the war but still feel themselves "losers."

For me, a pessimist about the South's chances for survival in recent years, the news is galvanizing. I am reading about it in *The New York Times* as I ride a bus down Fifth Avenue in Manhattan from my East Side apartment to the AP headquarters at 50 Rockefeller Plaza. I rush to the foreign desk on the fourth floor, where an editor thrusts news copy at me and says, "Look at this. Total chaos." I read a stream of information coming over the telex machine from our man in Saigon, George Esper, an indefatigable professional reporter I'd known for the 10 years he's been based in Vietnam. I tell Wes Gallagher that I believe the end is near and that I need to go there. Gallagher has spent much of his AP presidency involved in the Vietnam story, spending millions to obtain the best coverage. His reporters and photographers have won five Pulitzer Prizes. "Get over there," he tells me, "and we'll need a helluva lot more people joining you if you're right." I'm on my way the next day.

George Esper meets me at the Saigon airport, and tells me the government has just written off the northern quarter of the country, the provinces of Quang Tri and Thua Thien, including the old capital of Hue. I'm aware the Central Highlands are already gone, so South Vietnam is halved in a week. The Vietnamese people I know in Saigon are stunned and angry, realizing they are supporting a government that is continuing to stubbornly disregard the obvious arithmetic of the battlefield. They ask me where the Americans are, and where are the B-52 bombers that have rescued them in the past?

On March 24, I hitch a ride on an Air America courier flight to Danang, a city second only to Saigon, with a million people, and where the retreating defenders from abandoned cities to the north are regrouping. The U.S. Marines I saw wading ashore in 1965 fired their first shots here, and the city since has become what is commonly described as a bastion. I notice as I land the rows of sleek fighter-bombers and helicopters at the airport, on call to assist the many thousands of defenders in camps on the outskirts. But in town I see a city on the verge of collapse as crowds gather at intersections, arguing and shouting, and soldiers walk the streets aimlessly, their weapons at rest. The picture darkens as barges and boats carrying the bedraggled military evacuees from Hue pull into the harbor. The main streets of the docks are soon mobbed by half-dressed soldiers, their weapons discarded or lost, their shoulders bent in weariness.

I meet the American consul, Al Francis, who is hopeful that a planned airlift will soon fly tens of thousands of refugees to more secure locations in the south. That plan is soon quashed by the thump of exploding rockets that wakes me the next morning, the first shots fired by the communists against Danang. I marvel at the speed of the advance. Hue was 50 miles to the north and fell the previous day. Al Francis urges me and a few other reporters to hasten to the airport in a consulate van, and we push through crowds of people on the road heading in the same direction. By midmorning the terminal is crowded with men, women and children trying to leave. They are on the verge of hysteria, and mob the first plane to arrive, a chartered World Airways 727 we are booked to fly on. Airport security police begin shouting and firing their weapons in the air, and eventually push the crowds back, and I board the plane, grateful to be on my way back to Saigon to cover the worsening war as it moves closer to the nation's capital.

Three days later George Esper scoops his competitors with the news that Danang has fallen, but "thrown away" is a better term. A Vietnamese stringer photographer shows us his photographs of Danang's China Beach and Marble Mountain areas that tell the truth of what happened. Scores of large artillery guns and tanks, shipped to Vietnam from American supply arsenals to defend Danang, are abandoned on the yellow sands. Their guns point not to the mountain valleys from where the communist attackers are emerging, but nose down into the rippling waters of the South China Sea where their crews are swimming on inflated inner tubes to waiting rescue barges offshore.

In Washington, D.C., at this time, the Defense Department is blaming the lack of spare parts and insufficient bullets for the poor performance of the South Vietnamese military, and suggests Congress's growing coolness toward adequate financing is the source of the problem. But with several thousand Americans still working in Saigon in the defense attaché's office, officials have to know the sorry state of affairs. Morale is shockingly low in the Vietnamese army, and desertions have been growing over the previous two years. The billion dollars' worth of military equipment shipped to Vietnam by President Nixon to help win approval of the peace agreement was not accompanied by technicians who know how to use it. The United States has supplied more than 1,200 attack and transport planes to the Vietnamese by late 1973, making it the third largest air force in the world, but even then confidential Pentagon reports state that barely 50 percent of the planes are in working condition.

President Gerald Ford, endeavoring to put the government back together after President Nixon's resignation, looks to his secretary of state, Henry Kissinger, to handle the growing political embarrassment in Vietnam. In December 1973, Kissinger accepted the Nobel Prize for bringing peace and honor to Vietnam, and now there is no peace and little honor. Kissinger turns to his ambassador to Saigon, Graham Martin, to bear some of the burden. At home for medical reasons but ready to return to his post, Martin is called in late March to Kissinger's office for a meeting that includes the secretary's principal aides. In a long career in the State Department, Martin has gained the reputation of a skilled, loyal diplomat. He delayed his retirement to take up the Saigon post in 1973.

In a TV interview I have with Martin three years after the war, the ambassador recalls Kissinger telling him that day, "Well, we want to bid you Godspeed, you know. With the American propensity for the devil theory of history, we have to have someone out there to blame." If Kissinger is adroitly passing the buck to his ambassador, he succeeds. Martin takes him seriously. He tells me, "This was recognition on his part, and equally on my part, that this is the way the ball bounces. Whoever is in charge assumes a certain responsibility. Like the chap who rescued the little boy who fell off the dock, at great risk to himself, and finally brings him to his mother who says, 'Well, where is the cap he was wearing?' That sort of reaction is bound to happen."

Gallagher calls me back to the United States to address the annual membership meeting of the Associated Press in New Orleans in early April. I am offered a ride home by Ed Daley, the president of Oakland-based World Airways, often under charter by the U.S. government. Daley is a bulky, beret-wearing character straight out of an old silent action movie, with the pistol tucked into a leather belt around his thick middle adding to the impression. He has upset some of my colleagues with his habit of backing up some of his noisy dinner table arguments by drawing his weapon and smacking it on the table. I like his style, and admire his stated intention to save as many people as he can with his fleet of jets parked at Tan Son Nhut airport.

Daley doesn't let pesky regulations get in his way. He has gathered up 57 tiny babies from orphanages and from local families. A score of American civilians, the wives of government contractors anxious to go home, agree to tend to them on the long ride to safety. We assemble at a warehouse building far beyond the airport terminal, where a DC-8 cargo jet is discreetly parked in a darkened part of the building. I ask Daley why all the caution and he tells me, "Well, we got the permissions from local families to pick up the orphans, but the authorities are trying to tell me we can't leave without a lot of paperwork. So this will be a flight without the paperwork."

The chief pilot, Ken Healy, tells me of another complication, that our departure clearance has been denied because of a possible guerrilla attack on the airport. Daley brushes that aside, and orders we take off anyway. I go up to the cockpit and Daley hands me headphones. We taxi to the runway and accelerate. I hear the tower shouting, "Don't take off, don't take off. You have no clearance," but by the time the command is repeated for the third time we are in the air. I slide to the back of the plane with the orphans, many of them sleeping as the big jet soars farther into the sky, setting a course first for the Yokota airbase in Japan for refueling, and from there to Oakland, a 25-hour dash to freedom. Daley's dramatic flight makes large headlines in the United States and helps force officials to face up to the crisis and begin evacuating the most vulnerable people, and sooner rather than later, all Americans, from Saigon.

To the newspaper publishers in New Orleans I explain, "It is not easy to describe in these lovely surroundings in this lovely American city the total chaos that is enveloping the people of Saigon, who for better or worse participated in America's grand scheme to make South Vietnam a bulwark against the communism that is now overrunning it." I'm asked how long Saigon has left. I predict it will fall within the month. They seem stunned.

So is my wife, Nina, who explains that my mother, Jane, visiting us in New York at the time, can take care of our children while she accompanies me back to Saigon to take care of her own relatives. Nearly everyone we knew wants to leave because they fear that their connections to the earlier French authorities, and to the Americans, will imperil their future under a communist regime. My father-in-law once worked for the French colonial government, and was chief secretary to the Saigon National Assembly for a time. One brother-in-law is a senior logistics officer in the South Vietnamese army, the other an economic consultant to the current government. Within a week or two, fortunately, they are all able to leave.

Ambassador Martin has a major problem with handling a potential exodus of hundreds of thousands of Vietnamese who want to leave, while making sure the several thousands of Americans still in country are able to get out. He tells me after the war there was real danger of violence. "The feeling against Americans could have become a very dangerous thing. At this point General Loan, a police chief during the Tet uprising, had told one of our people that if you think you are going to march all the Americans to the airport and leave, you will find you are fighting us on the way out." General Loan is the Saigon police chief who early in the Tet Offensive of 1968 was caught by AP photographer Eddie Adams executing an alleged communist agent at point-blank range with his pistol.

Later widely criticized for his handling of the exodus, the ambassador explained to me after the war, "My preoccupation was to keep certain stability in Saigon. We did manage that. This meant you could not suddenly pull out all the police, even those who had been helpful to you. Although we had a responsibility to them you did not pull out all of the senior Vietnamese military, without whom there could be no continuity of command for the military cordon, which was formed around Saigon and ready to fight, and still with a considerable combat capability."

And as the powerful communist military machine that is capturing everything along the coast is preparing to wheel in from the east and west toward Saigon, the ambassador still has to deal with a desperate President Thieu, who remains adamant that America come to the rescue. A quick visit to Saigon is arranged for the last American force commander in Vietnam, General Frederick Weyand, who agrees to recommend to President Ford many hundreds of millions more dollars in financial aid. But no further aid materializes.

For a week or so, hopes and Vietnamese pride are raised by the valiant last stand of the South Vietnamese 18th Infantry Division at Xuan Loc, a provincial center, 50 miles east of Saigon. Xuan Loc holds the key to the gates of Saigon, anchoring the last defensive line that runs in an arc from the Cambodian border to the South China Sea. The 18th Division is the last of President Thieu's final reserve, and he names it the Supermen Division as he sends it into action against the formidable communist juggernaut that so far has swept everything before it.

Surprising many, the 18th holds. I travel with other reporters to the battle scene a week into the action, our journey beginning badly when we realize the bus driver taking us to our helicopter departure point 15 miles away is crazily drunk. At Xuan Loc we meet the commander, General Le Minh Dao, at his makeshift headquarters amid the tangle of shell-wrecked buildings and destroyed vehicles. The roar of mortars and the crack of machine-gun fire rend the smoke-filled air as the daring general flatly vows to continue stalling the enemy advance, to try and hold on until death. Saigon's last effective elite marine and ranger units are on their way to help. The Vietnamese air force is also defying anti-aircraft fire with numerous bombing and strafing runs against the enemy.

As we depart on a large transport helicopter sent in especially for us, several dozen local people fight to get on board, and are shoved back by rifle butt–wielding security men. The stubborn resistance at Xuan Loc forces the North Vietnamese commanders to change their final plan, directing units committed elsewhere to the unexpected battle, ordering them to "open the gates" to Saigon. The 18th Division holds on from April 9 to April 21, a heroic 13 days still remembered with pride by the uprooted Vietnamese living in the United States.

President Thieu is advised by his senior commanders that the fall of Xuan Loc has wiped out any further attempts to resist. Ambassador Martin also visits him, to hint broadly that it is time for him to go. Thieu resigns the next morning and flies off with a planeload of his possessions to Taiwan. In his interview in London, Thieu reveals his lasting bitterness toward the United States. "They abandoned us. They sold us out. They stabbed us in the back. It's true, they betrayed us. A great ally failed a small ally."

The CIA agent who escorted Thieu to the airport has a different assessment. "Thieu was far too tolerant of corruption. He was a weak leader. He made countless military errors for which lesser men would be drawn and quartered," says Frank Snepp in an interview with me after the war. "But all that being said, he was lied to by the U.S. government."

With Thieu gone, and thousands more jeopardized Vietnamese still to be evacuated, a flurry of wishful thinking pervades American officials in both Saigon and Washington. They begin to hope that the emergence of a nonaligned political leader in Saigon might persuade the North Vietnamese to end their military assault and accept some kind of political arrangement that will guarantee the neutrality of the city. The source of these fallacious ideas, reported seriously in some mainstream American newspapers, is apparently the French Embassy in Saigon and Russian diplomats trusted by Henry Kissinger in Washington. The appointment as president on April 28 of the aging General Duong Van Minh, the man who led the coup d'état against Ngo Dinh Diem in 1963, is seen to be the ideal choice to bring such a deal to fruition. But an hour after he makes his first official speech calling for peace, captured South Vietnamese fighter-bombers flown by communist pilots make several bombing runs against the city. It is the North Vietnamese response to the wishful thinkers.

Frank Snepp is the senior CIA analyst in the embassy at that time. He learns through a classified intelligence system that General Van Tien Dung, his forces now firmly in control around the whole of Saigon, has begun thinking that the evacuation delay is deliberate. Snepp tells me, "He radios his field commanders. He thinks we are trying to pull a fast one, trying to hold up the evacuation, to buy time. He orders that if the Americans are not out of Saigon by 6 o'clock this evening, his people must use their artillery to blast the center of the city." Snepp remembers that "panic reigned in the embassy that night."

Officials did not pass on the threat information to the dozens of foreign journalists still working in Saigon. Within a few hours, they would find out for themselves what was on the impatient mind of General Dung.

CONCLUSION

WAR ENDS, BUT
VIETNAM STILL CALLS

T HE FALL OF SAIGON, ending South Vietnam's
20-year struggle for survival, comes with
unforeseen suddenness, as I describe in the opening
chapter of this book. An overwhelming blitz by the
enemy, a chaotic scramble to evacuate by vulnerable
Vietnamese and Americans still in the capital, then
looting and a strange calm: All of this plays out before
my eyes in a final, surreal day of this war.

The assault that brings this conclusion begins
with an early morning bombardment of Saigon's
Tan Son Nhut airport on April 29, ordered by the commander of North Vietnamese military forces, General Van Tien Dung. His tanks then quickly roll in to
take over the city. In the countryside, the few South
Vietnamese military forces still reasonably well organized see further combat as pointless, either because
of the overwhelming power of the communists' heavy

weaponry brought against them, or by the collapse of
political will in Saigon.

Thirty-five miles north of Saigon, the high drama
of the North Vietnamese military campaign unfolds
at Lai Khe, home base of the 1st Infantry Division,
President Thieu's old outfit. The unit has guarded
vulnerable Route 13, but is sidelined now because the
lightning attack on Saigon comes from other directions. With his unit's capabilities still intact, the division commander, Brigadier General Le Nguyen Vy,
begins weighing his options, according to surviving
officers I meet in Saigon a week or so later. His military command headquarters is not responding to his
messages, however, and he is relying on Radio Saigon news broadcasts for tactical information. It was
at this location, Lai Khe, where a brigade of the U.S.
1st Infantry Division was based during the American
war, that I made the acquaintance of its innovative
commander, Major General William DePuy, in 1966.
His massive helicopter assaults on the enemy made
military history. But there are no helicopters to assist
General Vy today.

General Vy decides to regroup all units, in preparation to move the whole division south to Saigon to
join in the fight. But by early morning of April 30 the
fight is clearly over, as Saigon Radio reports communist troops moving toward downtown. At 7 a.m., General Vy calls a staff meeting. All are present except the

```
APB473
    381

  U R G E N T

  SURRENDER (TOPS)

  (SAIGON) - SOUTH VIETNAM TONIGHT ANNOUNCED ITS UNCONDITIONAL

SURRENDER TO THE VIET CONG.

  THE ANNOUNCEMENT WAS MADE BY PRESIDENT DUONG VAN ''BIG'' MINH WHO

SAID IN A RADIO SPEECH ADDRESSED TO THE VIET CONG:

  ''WE ARE HERE TO HAND OVER TO YOU THE POWER IN ORDER TO AVOID

BLOODSHED.''

  HE ORDERED THE SOUTH VIETNAMESE ARMY TO STOP FIRING - AND TO

REMAIN IN PLACE.

  10:35PED   04-29-75
```

Wire copy filed as an "Urgent" to New York by AP Saigon bureau chief George Esper on Apr. 29, 1975. It reads:

URGENT. Surrender (TOPS). (Saigon)—South Vietnam tonight announced its unconditional surrender to the Viet Cong. The announcement was made by President Duong Van "Big" Minh who said in a radio speech addressed to the Viet Cong: "We are here to hand over to you the power in order to avoid bloodshed." He ordered the South Vietnamese Army to stop firing—and to remain in place.

(AP Corporate Archives)

Second wire copy filed as an "Urgent" from AP Saigon bureau chief George Esper on Apr. 29, 1975. It reads:

> URGENT. Surrender (take 2). The surrender came only hours after Americans had left Saigon in an armada of helicopters guarded by some 800 Marines. The evacuating Americans had dodged random shots fired by bitter South Vietnamese soldiers and had fought off desperate civilians. Viet Cong gunners had sent rockets into Saigon's Tan Son Nhut (Tahn Suhn Yuht) air base as a rear guard of American Marines had been evacuated from the rooftop of the abandoned US embassy in downtown Saigon. The shelling continued. And the Viet Cong claimed they had captured the big Bien Hoa (Byen Hwah) air base 15 miles north of the capital. Then came the announcement from Saigon: unconditional surrender.

(AP Corporate Archives)

deputy division commander, who has fled in an American plane. Vy turns the command of his division over to Colonel Tu Van, and tells them Saigon will soon fall, and adds, "As an officer of the South Vietnamese army I must act for the honor of the army, but you must protect the lives of the soldiers. Good luck to you all." He returns to his quarters, lights a cigarette, takes his pistol and blows his brains out.

General Vy is buried with full military honors, the whole division assembled at the Lai Khe flagpole. A participating officer later tells me it was "a short but emotional service, his body buried, and the honor of the division is saved." At 1 p.m. that day, after hearing of the government's surrender, the division boards 200 trucks and drives over to the town of Ben Cat, newly occupied by the communists. The soldiers dismount, drop their weapons and take off their uniforms as about 50 enemy soldiers carrying Russian AK-47 rifles stand watching them. They stay for two days under guard at Ben Cat, and then all but the officers are released to their families.

The collapse of South Vietnam is noted for what didn't happen as well as for what did. For weeks some American officials in Saigon are warning of a probable "bloodbath" against the population if vengeful communist soldiers are let loose, citing reports from the 16 provinces captured in the first six weeks of the offensive. Young embassy aides lobby journalists with tales of "horrendous crimes" and hand out pink copies of reports to Washington claiming the execution of 300 soldiers and policemen on the streets of Ban Me Thuot, and the wholesale killing of half-American babies in the coastal city of Nhatrang. The Saigon government will say only that it has "some confirming reports."

But in an enterprising North Vietnamese initiative to discredit the accusations, several American journalists are invited to Danang where brutalities are allegedly being committed. A former AP senior executive, Dan De Luce, who won a Pulitzer Prize for his World War II reporting, and his wife Alma, a photographer, accept the invitation and fly in from New York. Their stories for the AP report on a calm Danang returning to normal. I challenge one persistent embassy official, whom I have known for 10 years, to tell me the truth. He acknowledges there is a political motive: "Well, honestly, we are making a lot of this issue because it can affect ongoing deliberations of the aid program here. We know some congressmen are already wavering to our side," which is for the approval of a substantial financial package. The vigorous fear campaign helps panic Saigon's already nervous population. Within a few weeks after the war's end, at least 1,000 of the Vietnamese evacuees who fought their way out of the country on American aircraft and Navy transports are petitioning officials at the holding camps in Guam to return them home.

The North Vietnamese do have a punishing blueprint for their vanquished enemy, primarily an extensive program of re-education camps, which will eventually imprison hundreds of thousands of military and political opponents, sent to live precariously in remote parts of the country. Some remain incarcerated for years, including Brigadier General Ly Ba Hy, a 25-year veteran of the South Vietnamese army who, upon his release in 1987, writes a book titled, "My 4,584 Days of Re-education in Vietnam." He will die in Paris in February 2015.

Another imprisoned officer is one I meet over the years, Major General Ly Tong Ba, the protégée of my friend the American warrior John Paul Vann. The Vietnamese officer's outstanding generalship of the South Vietnamese 23rd Infantry Division contributes to decisive victory in the 1972 battle of Kontum, the same action where Vann is killed. In the defense of the western route into Saigon in the last days of the war in 1975, General Ba commands the 25th Infantry Division in a fight to the finish. His unit is relentlessly pounded by heavy communist artillery and tank fire, ominously echoing the enormous American Air Force B-52 bomber strikes used in his defense of Kontum three years earlier. I learn later from officers in Saigon that Ba ordered his headquarters' unit at Cu Chi to hold, allowing a retreat of his surviving few hundred soldiers in the last hours of the war. He is caught about to escape across a nearby river as surrender is being announced in Saigon. The victorious communists do not view him with the same unabashed adoration felt for him by Vietnamese who seek to find honor in their defeat. General Ba is sent to imprisonment in a distant re-education camp, where for 13 years political cadres endeavor to quell his spirit. He is finally released in March 1988, white haired and weak but, according to his friends, unbroken. Within a year he arrives in the United States; he'll die in February 2015 in Las Vegas with family around him.

The abuses of the re-education camps help fuel the unremitting bitterness of the vast majority of America's Vietnamese veterans, who see April 30 not as the day of liberation as celebrated by the communist victors but as a date in a Black April that ruined their lives.

In Saigon immediately after the war's end, the authorities allow us visiting newspeople to move around freely for a few days. Then they begin tightening controls, opening up international communications but restricting travel and closely censoring our stories. All bookstores and magazine stalls close after a government order prohibiting the sale or possession of any literature published under the former regime, a tit-for-tat response to the prior banning of all pro-communist literature. I notice that many soldiers are moving into houses around the city center, particularly those left behind by the evacuees. Sixteen soldiers occupy a house owned by my departed Vietnamese in-laws, where I had lived off and on for the previous 14 years. The soldiers' leader explains, "Our policy is to cohabit with the people." Then he asks that I give up my room. My days here now are clearly winding down. I present my white Karmann Ghia sports car, which served me well in covering the war in the early years, to our loyal office assistant, Huan, an eager, diminutive man who is not evacuated with the rest of our local staff. That's because it turns out he is a polygamist, with two families, one separate from the other, and he can't decide which one to take.

Along with most of the press corps, I leave on May 24 on a Russian-built Ilyushin aircraft with Hanoi's yellow-striped red flag painted on the tail. The night before my departure, I am summoned to the Saigon *Giai Phong* (Liberation) newspaper, the only publication now allowed in town. The editor greets me warmly and says, "I have read your dispatches while I was in the jungle, Mr. Arnett. I welcome you to the new Vietnam. Everything is perfect, isn't it?" His comments have the moral certainty I've found in the views of most of the communist officials I've met in my three-week stay in the new Vietnam. I don't argue with him. The days of arguing in South Vietnam seem over for good.

I believe I've put Vietnam behind me when I return to New York City in May 1975, and the AP gives me many other interesting assignments, including several weeks in India in 1976 when Prime Minister Indira Gandhi is drawing criticism over her repressive rule. But Vietnam will keep tugging me back, like a boat trying to put out to sea while still tied to the dock. The election of Jimmy Carter as America's 39th president in 1976 comes as Americans are endeavoring to recover from the war and from the Watergate scandal, and he quickly moves with a new initiative to end what he describes as the "Vietnam malaise." In a foreign policy speech early in 1977, he says, "For too many years we've been willing to adopt the flawed and erroneous principles of our adversaries, sometimes abandoning our own values for theirs. We've fought fire with fire, never thinking that fire is sometimes best quenched with water. This approach failed, with Vietnam the best example of its intellectual and moral poverty. But through failure we have now found our way back to our own principles and values, and we have regained our lost confidence."

Carter appoints a presidential commission to Vietnam in March 1977, less than two months after he takes office, its purpose to pursue rapid diplomatic relations with the former enemy and begin resolving a growing controversy over American servicemen still missing in the old war zones. Heading the commission is the president of the United Auto Workers union, Leonard Woodcock, a senior statesman of the American labor movement, also noted for his resistance to the Vietnam War (which had earned him ninth place on President Nixon's infamous enemies list). Also included in the commission is Senate Majority Leader Mike Mansfield, whom I had first met in a hotel room in Saigon in December 1962, where we discussed the problems of the Ngo Dinh Diem regime. I am one of five reporters chosen to go along on this trip with the commission, the first American journalists to visit Vietnam since the war ended nearly two years earlier.

We leave Washington, D.C., on a presidential jet on March 13, arriving in Hanoi 13 hours later. Word reaches us that if our motorcade gets bogged down in traffic on our way into town it will be a sign of the Vietnamese government viewing the commission with disfavor. We roll straight through. The atmosphere in Hanoi is very different from that on my trip in late 1972, when I visited with an anti-war group and U.S warplanes were still bombing the outskirts of the city. The few people we saw on the streets then were poorly dressed and slight of build. This time I see a city rejuvenating with busier streets and more food in the stores. Peace has clearly brought its bonuses to the victorious north. We are housed at a new five-story hotel on Ngo Quyen Street, much to the envy of resident diplomats who are living in the ancient

Unification Hotel around the corner. They tell us our accommodation is the most comfortable in town.

Woodcock is matched against the deputy foreign minister, Phan Hien, in his negotiations, a five-day marathon that he later describes as the toughest in his career. He brings a unique perspective to the talks, a private citizen rather a professional diplomat. He tells us over a beer the first evening that, "if a State Department official had been here with me he would have died a thousand deaths. I emphasized that our two countries were meeting as equals. I told him that this is the best group they would ever get from America, with men of stature like Mike Mansfield. I told him that if they closed the door on us then it might take 10 more years before we are back."

The Vietnamese official tells him, "You will not be disappointed." By week's end the remains of 12 missing Americans pilots are handed over to the commission, a few of the 795 servicemen still listed as missing by the Defense Department. Hanoi also agrees to set up an office to receive information about the missing servicemen, but on an understanding that the group will take back home the Vietnamese view that American aid and reconstruction for the war-torn country are required as "a question of humanitarian principle." Unlike in my last days in Saigon in May 1975, officials here are cooperative, my stories moving swiftly to New York without censorship.

Meeting with Prime Minister Pham Van Dong just prior to our departure, Woodcock again plays the concerned private citizen, and tells him, "Speaking personally as an American, we being here is like rolling the clock back to 1945, a time when the United States based its policies on the support of allies in Europe rather than the aspirations of people here. Now we can start over again."

We fly out of Hanoi to Clark Air Force Base in the Philippines, where a big C-141 StarLifter aircraft is waiting to load the remains of the recovered servicemen. Watching the uniformed aircrew reverently loading the steel caskets into the interior of the plane is Dr. Roger Shields, a consultant to the Pentagon on POW affairs. He tells me, "I'm remembering something from four years ago, when we were welcoming the released American prisoners of war arriving here at Clark. They were alive and joyful that day, they were going home. And so these boys are going home, too."

President Carter never does get his Vietnam policy off the ground. His administration tries hard, withholding its veto on Vietnam's admittance to the United Nations, but both houses of Congress flatly refuse to provide aid to the Hanoi government. And the missing prisoner of war question blows up into a passionate political issue that takes years to resolve. The man who led the Vietnam mission, Leonard Woodcock, in 1979 becomes the first American ambassador to a China under communist rule.

Vietnam fades as an American foreign policy issue, but the human suffering cannot be ignored. Thousands of discontented Vietnamese take to the seas beginning two years after the war, seeking refuge in any other country that will take them. They are the boat people whose privations on their long voyages in often unseaworthy ships shock the world. Their suffering is worsened by the depredations of Thai pirates, who emerge from the thousands of legitimate fishing boats in the Gulf of Thailand to brutally rape, steal from and kidnap as many as 30 percent of the seafarers, according to United Nations estimates.

In 1978, AP photographer Eddie Adams and I set out on a four-continent assignment to write about the world's 10 million homeless people. On the advice of a human rights activist friend, we travel to the Malaysian island of Bidong, once a paradise with blue waters, white sandy beaches fringed by coconut palms, topped by a verdant hillside. We were told it was a haven for boat people. What we find is a tropical Skid Row, home to 30,000 desperate Vietnamese on a 100-acre slice of land that has been reduced to a living hell. A putrid odor assails us as we step off the ferry boat from Kuala Terengganu, the nearest mainland port two hours away. We are told there are no toilets on the island other than what nature provides on the rocks, hillsides and low-tide beaches.

We see the latest arrivals, a small red boat with 11 bedraggled people on board trying to land at the beach, but Malaysian marine police will not let them in immediately. Watching them, Nguyen Phong Lau, 33, who says he is a former interpreter for the U.S. Provost Marshals in Saigon, recalls his own arrival there on the evening of Jan. 9. "When me and the 60 others on the boat land at the beach we are set upon by young Malaysians armed with knives, who take everyone's wallets and watches and most of the food. And then they tried to push us back into the water until police arrived to help."

Rutted dirt paths lead from the filthy beaches through a shantytown of small dwellings made of cardboard boxes, straw mats and tree branches. The people we see, particularly the many children, look thin and unhealthy. We are told there are 2,500 orphans on the island. The Reverend Nguyen Xan Bao of the Christian Reformed Church holds classes for several hundred of them, and he explains why there are so many. "Their mothers in Vietnam told them to go down to the beach and play. You might get a trip to America, they are told, and they hitch rides from passing boats." Dr. Nguyen Van Hong, 34, is a general practitioner who also helps with social services. His office has lost its wooden back wall since there was no other available material to build a coffin for an old man who had died of asthma. Dr. Hong says people here are on the verge of starvation.

We see Vuong Kiet Khiem scaling up the hillside with his ax and his three oldest children. He is looking for the tough stumpy trees that can be sold to make crude furniture. He's a 39-year-old Chinese-Vietnamese merchant expelled from Saigon for no reason, he says. He paid 50 ounces of gold, all the money he possessed, to flee with his wife and eight children. Others remember the pirates with bitterness. Tran Thi Qui tells me she was on boat KGO 480 that left Soctrang the previous November. They were attacked by pirates six times during the seven-day journey, she said, "and the last band took everyone's clothing because there was nothing else left to steal."

A former pop singer, Thanh Tuyen, had a safer journey. She serves coffee for two dollars a cup in her shack beside the beach. Popular in Saigon for her 1977 hit song, "Heat Up My Revolutionary Fires, Darling," she fled to find a more appreciative audience than the rustic cadre who sipped tea and giggled at her rarely permitted public performances at home.

With the permission of the Malaysian authorities, the refugees established a primitive government on the island, including a judicial system. In the early afternoon we watch Dr. Trong Buu Hoa, the camp commander, receive a couple at his shack he calls City

Hall, where he declares them married. He offers to write a certificate, but it's useful only as a souvenir and they don't bother. He says he has married a dozen so far. "It's not the Vietnamese way, it's the refugee way," he explains. Where does a couple go for a honeymoon on such a crowded island? Dr. Hoa points to a flat rock, the "lovers' rock," 600 feet up the hill. And he said there is also the deep water of the bay beyond where people frolic.

The boat people who stream from Vietnam to neighboring countries such as Thailand, Malaysia, Singapore, Indonesia and even as far as Australia, 8,000 miles away, come from many strata of society. They include members of the old military who are viewed as pariahs in the new Vietnam, politicians in a one-party state, businessmen denied bank financing, disaffected youth, and farmers and fishermen who get entangled in the bureaucracy of a government-controlled economy. Up until a few months ago no one lived on Bidong. The Malaysian government decided to dump unwanted arrivals here rather than on the mainland. With bitter humor the refugees call it "Bidat," which means terrible in Vietnamese. Many will stay for a year or more. Only a few hundred have left so far, even though officials from the American and Australian embassies visit to seek suitable candidates for resettlement. Bidong is low on the list because of the priorities given to older camps farther down the Malaysian coast.

As Adams and I prepare to depart Bidong on the last ferry of the day, we hear the tune of a familiar hymn, "Jesu, Joy of Man's Desiring," being sung in Chinese. We head up to what someone tells us is the Catholic church, a large crude structure on the hillside. Branches form the frame; two hand-hewn posts support what passes as the altar. A khaki-colored plastic tent is the roof; sugar and flour bags are the walls. A rough wooden cross stands on the nearby headland. A children's choir is practicing hymns for the Sunday service. Nearby there's a simple painted sign, "Bidong, a way station to a better life."

In April 1979, four other reporters and I return to Vietnam with United Nations Secretary-General Kurt Waldheim on an official visit to Asian capitals. We use a luxury jet aircraft from the fleet of President Ferdinand Marcos of the Philippines to make the trip, and arrive in Hanoi to a changed world. Two months earlier the Chinese army invaded the northern border in retaliation for Vietnam's overthrow of the Chinese-backed Khmer Rouge government of Cambodia in 1978. In six determined drives into Vietnam with troops supported by armor and artillery, the Chinese caused considerable damage, particularly to the border towns of Langson and Dong Dang.

In my first story for the AP this time from Hanoi, remembering my visit there in 1972 during the American air war, I write, "The clock is turned back seven years. It is a time of war. But the enemy is not the United States; it is Vietnam's longtime ally, China, now being called an aggressor in newspapers and street posters." I see that the curbside air raid shelters, filled in when the Saigon regime collapsed in 1975, have been redug and are ready for use. Two wall-sized posters have been painted side by side in a Hanoi street. One shows an American pilot with bowed head walking at the point of a gun held by a young woman. It is labeled "1972." The other portrait shows a Chinese soldier with a peaked cap also walking at the point of a gun held by a woman. It is labeled "1979." Beside each are dozens of pictures of war damage and dead and wounded in the same years. In a visit in 1977, I had noticed that attractive Reunification Park was a popular locale for young lovers, but on this visit I see groups of young boys and girls practicing weapons maintenance and military drills. An official guide explains, "We are training everywhere in the parks and the fields to be prepared against the Chinese." In 1972, similar drills were held in the park to prepare for an American invasion.

I see something similar when the U.N. secretary-general visits Saigon a few days later. As in Hanoi, people here see the American war passing quickly into history, unlike in the United States, where emotions are continuing to run high at this time. One explanation is the single-mindedness of purpose that characterized the war against the Americans. The Vietnamese authorities are now alerting the population to the new enemy, China. I ask a young man, Le Manh Minh, exercising in a park, what he thinks about the American war. "It was a bad war, but our enemy is China now."

My return to Saigon is a poignant one. I invested years of my life covering the Vietnam War story. The city looks the same on the surface, but there are changes. John F. Kennedy Square beside the cathedral is now Paris Commune Place. The National Assembly Building has returned to its original purpose, an opera house. And all the bars have closed. I run into Huan, our office boy at the AP Saigon bureau during the war years. He is a street photographer now, working for a hole-in-the-wall photo shop to support his two families. Huan says local officials are trying the confiscate the sports car I gave him four years earlier. He begs me to send him the ownership papers that I had long ago lost.

There is a brass plaque recently placed on the front wall of the abandoned U.S. Embassy building, the scene of so much mayhem four years earlier as the last Americans scrambled onto helicopters to avoid the approaching communist military tsunami. The plaque reads: "On April 29, 1975, top American and puppet government leaders departed by helicopter from this building and thereby put an end to the American war of aggression in Vietnam."

The U.N.'s Waldheim finds on this visit that the Vietnamese are not interested in his offer to help resolve the differences with China, with Prime Minister Pham Van Dong telling him, "We can handle them ourselves." Waldheim again tries a mediator role eight days later when we fly on to Beijing and he meets with the Chinese leader Deng Xiaoping, who had earlier ordered the military invasion of his neighboring fellow communist nation. I photograph them together at the Forbidden City, where previous Chinese emperors had ruled in splendor. There stands Deng, the diminutive Chinese revolutionary who has outlived and outmaneuvered Mao Zedong, and the tall, elegant Austrian aristocrat who runs the U.N. Deng is smiling confidently. He is launching his far-reaching plans for the economic transformation of China. As for Vietnam, he tells Waldheim, "I admire my brother revolutionaries, but they need to be taught a lesson occasionally." The U.N. leader nods diplomatically, realizing there is nothing much he can do about it.

Years later, in the 2000s, when I'm teaching journalism at Shantou University in southern China, I take a dozen of my best students on a three-week educational visit to Vietnam where they see cities bursting with fevered economic development and modern skylines, just as in their cities back home. Vietnam is now an economic tiger, its Marxist yoke thrown over for capitalism. With diplomatic relations having been reopened with the Hanoi government by President Bill Clinton in the 1990s and with its big neighbor China continuing to growl menacingly, the U.S. military, once the enemy to Vietnam, is looking more like a partner.

With my students, I plan to visit some of the old Vietnam battlefields, because I've talked to my senior classes about press coverage of the war. In an exhausting, long, hot day north of Hue spent mostly walking, I first take my students to the Truong Son National Cemetery, where 10,000 North Vietnamese soldiers are buried, many of them killed defending the Ho Minh Trail infiltration route during the American war. A mile or so farther east, on a small hill amid tangled prickly vines, rotted sandbags and bits of rusted metal and garbage, is the old U.S. Marine firebase of Con Thien.

We trudge along a narrow trail, careful not to stumble on unexploded shells, which have killed or injured many local farmers. We arrive at the one surviving feature of the old base, a square strongpoint of crumbling concrete, its outer walls pockmarked with shell and bullet holes, and inside, as centipedes and spiders run for cover, we see on the moss-covered walls scribbled American names and patriotic sayings.

Con Thien was tactically important because it was located a little more than a mile away from the Vietnamese demilitarized zone and overlooked communist activities just across the border. In an impromptu classroom beside the old, battered building, I tell my students how for a whole year from early 1967 the communists threw artillery shells, rockets, and human wave attacks against Con Thien; in one action alone 44 Marines died, along with more than 100 North Vietnamese. I tell them of the harrowing three days I spent there in a visit, cringing in foxholes as the battle raged. Con Thien held throughout the onslaughts.

My students, young women all, look attentively at me, some wearing the colorful clothes modeled on the then-popular American TV shows "Sex and the City" and "Gossip Girl" that they watch on the Internet in their dorms. They are looking now at me, at an aged war reporter in baggy clothes, telling war stories again, and wiping sweat from his face with a handful of disintegrating Kleenex tissues. One of them, Hewitt, who is wearing a T-shirt stamped with the phrase "Scary Random Bombing," asks me, "You mean to tell us that young American boys came all this way to this place to fight and die. Why?" I offer no quick answer to her question. And in thinking about it later I realize I had no answer that would have made any sense to them.

ACKNOWLEDGEMENTS

Tᴴɪꜱ ᴡʀɪᴛɪɴɢ ᴀꜱꜱɪɢɴᴍᴇɴᴛ has been one of the most satisfying in my 55-year career as a journalist, and for that I have to thank the Associated Press news organization. They asked me to write this personal account of the Vietnam War to resonate with a younger audience far removed from that era, and to recall for my own generation the drama and controversy we lived through for the many years that war lasted. It was a challenging task, one I undertook knowing that the Vietnam War still stirs argument in the United States, but a task made easier by the enthusiasm of management and staff of The Associated Press.

The AP I know well, having covered the Vietnam War for the news organization from 1962 to the Fall of Saigon in 1975. It never let me down in all those years, and in this project, too, the editorial, photographic and research staff willingly provided the necessary assistance to meet our tight deadlines. The AP's Digital Publishing Specialist Peter Costanzo was my primary contact and he was unfailingly supportive. I relied on Chris Sullivan, editor of AP's National

Reporting Team, for daily commentary and consultation as we moved through the assignment chapter by chapter. Valerie Komor, Director of Corporate Archives, has long been a custodian of the reportage and memorabilia of her news organization's Vietnam era, and her help—along with the expert assistance of Processing Archivist Francesca Pitaro—was invaluable.

Particularly helpful to me in this project were acquaintances in the Vietnamese diaspora who settled in the United States after the communist victory ended their hopes of establishing a democratic South Vietnam. A friend of many years, Nguyen Ngoc Linh, provided me valuable insights into the difficult readjustment required by those who appreciated America's open arms in welcoming them here, but still dream of what could have been in their former homeland. The Information Minister at a critical time, Hoang Duc Nha, provided me with a vivid account of his dealings with Henry Kissinger and President Nguyen Van Thieu which helped clarify the political confusion of the last years of the war.

My own family, long accustomed to my absences at war fronts over the years, encouraged me from the beginning to accept this project, knowing that of all the conflicts I have covered, the Vietnam War was the most influential personally and historically. My son Andrew, a journalist himself, made perceptive appraisals of the written material I emailed him regularly, while my wife Nina and daughter Elsa were closer at hand and always supportive.

APPENDIX

PETER ARNETT:
AN ORAL HISTORY

Jan. 30, 2006

The Associated Press Oral History Program
Interview conducted by Valerie S. Komor,
Director, AP Corporate Archives

KOMOR: Good afternoon, Peter. I'm here with Peter Arnett at the headquarters of The Associated Press; it is Monday, January 30th, 2006, and Peter and I are going to chat about his time at The Associated Press. But, Peter, tell me first, where were you when you became a stringer for the AP? Was that your first job at the AP?

ARNETT: Yes, I was a reporter for the *Bangkok World* newspaper in Bangkok from 1958 to early 1960. And during that period, when really there was very little interest in Asia from the part of the United States, very few AP reporters were in Asia at that point. There was one reporter at the AP bureau, Tony Escoda was his name, a Filipino-American, really bright young man, and he employed me to do some stringing work. When he couldn't get out of the office, he'd call me, and I would do stories on the political situation; occasionally interviewed visiting celebrities. And was—that's where I really began my association. 1958.

Two years after that, early in 1960, I went to live in Vientiane in Laos, because the *Bangkok World* newspaper had started a Sunday newspaper called the *Vientiane World*. They were trying to develop a market in Vientiane, which is the capital of Laos, which had a large American community at that point, a couple of thousand diplomats, military people. It seemed to be a, a, you know, a potential market, certainly, for advertising and readership. So I agreed to go up to edit this paper in Vientiane. It turned out that I was one of two reporters who lived there; there was an AFP correspondent and me. There was no one else. Whereas in Bangkok, which was a much more flourishing city, it was commonplace for reporters to come through; there were reporters based there. Little Laos had no one, even though at that time, Laos was becoming the center of attention for the United States. In fact, when President John F. Kennedy was elected, and had a—his first long meeting with Dwight Eisenhower, the outgoing president, Eisenhower reportedly told him, you know, "Don't worry about Vietnam. Laos is going to be the center of your problems. Because Laos—the communist Chinese are building a road through the northern area; you've got a communist revolutionary group called the Pathet Lao that are developing, and we've got a pro-American military government in Vientiane that you have to support." So, even though it was becoming the center of attention within the U.S. government, generally it was looked upon as sort of a quiet, lost little place. And it was there in Laos where I further cemented my relationship with the AP, because I was the AP correspondent there, they didn't have any local person. So they called upon me to cover events for them. There weren't a lot of events, but when they did happen, they would message me, and I would cover the initial newsbreaks, and if necessary, they'd send in correspondents from Hong Kong or Bangkok or Tokyo, depending on how big the story got. But I would be the first, you know, the first source that they would use.

KOMOR: And how long did you do that, Peter?

ARNETT: I was there for the rest of the year, basically. And the operation of the *Vientiane World*, plus the U.S. political military operation was to end later that year, because there was a coup d'état by a disaffected battalion commander of the royal Lao military. His name was Captain Kong Le; he had a paratroop battalion.

He hadn't been paid for months; he got so angry that he pulled a coup d'état in Vientiane, and took over the government. Even though I had known Kong Le, and drank a few beers with him [laughs] earlier that year, he called me in and said, "Well, the *Vientiane World* is financed by the CIA; get out of town." It wasn't financed by the CIA, but the CIA assistant station chief's wife worked for the mag—for the publication as a gossip columnist. So, they were half right. So I left at that point. Now, that coup d'état also solidified my relationship with the AP. Because—Vientiane, Laos, was the back of beyond in terms of communication in 1960. There was a post office with a very tenuous phone connection to the outside world. But when the coup d'état came, that phone connection stopped. Now, in earlier crises, we'd been able to go to the U.S. Embassy and use their transmission lines to get at least, sort of, a small paragraph or two out. But because of this coup d'état, the embassy was very embarrassed; they were frightened; they wouldn't let us in the embassy. So I had no recourse but to file my story in Thailand where you had post offices in the border region, which is just across the Mekong River from Vientiane, that we could file our stories. You could pay them money, and they would telex them. But you did have the Mekong River as a barrier, it was a mile across. Part of it was sandy; part of it was open

current. So I just took off one morning with the AP
story, swam across the river...

KOMOR: Where did you put the story while you were
swimming?

ARNETT: Hitched a ride on a truck, from the little
village across from Vientiane to Udorn, which was
about 60 miles south. Filed the story, and got a beat. I
remember the San Francisco Chronicle had a headline
on Page 3, "The First Dispatch From the War-Torn
Laotian Area" by Peter Arnett, and I don't—I did that
in successive days, but I started taking news stories
for *The New York Times*, because they had arrived; for
a couple of other papers, plus AP. And I think that
impressed the AP, as certainly my derring-do. It also
impressed the AP senior executive for the area, a man
called Don Huth, who ran the Southeast Asian operation out of Singapore. So Don, whom I'd bumped
into a few times, a few months later talked to me, and
asked me if I was sort of interested in getting more
permanent employment. And I did have mixed feelings at the time, because I sort of returned to my
dream about going to Fleet Street. And this was rein-
forced by having met various British correspondents
who had come through: *The Daily Mirror*, the *Daily
Express*. And they were just gung-ho, party guys. You

know, they—whereas American journalists were serious, looking for the facts, these Britishers...

KOMOR: Did not appeal to you. They, they appealed to you.

ARNETT: Yeah, they wanted to tell colorful stories, and they, and they—and I sort of figured, "Hey, this is sort of more my style." So, I remember asking one of them from the Daily Express, a man who I'd gotten to know because I had been also stringing for the Daily Express, I asked him about recommending me to the paper in London. Because I said, "I want to go to London; I've saved some money, and I want to work for the Daily Express." And he said, "Sure, I'll recommend you." But he says, "You know what's going to happen? You'll go to London. They'll hire you. And if you're really good, after five years, they'll send you right back here. Why leave? Stay here." And on that advice, I looked around for work, and ultimately got the offer from Don Huth to go to Indonesia, midyear in '61, to be the correspondent in Indonesia for the AP. It was a local hire arrangement; I was being reasonably well paid by local standards. But it was sort of a local hire, so on that basis, for example, I paid my own fare down to Jakarta. The AP wouldn't come up with the money. What I actually did, I got a ride on Thai Airways and wrote a puff piece for their magazine to cover the cost of the fare. Just one other story I'll tell you in Vientiane, Laos. I mentioned earlier, I was the only correspondent. The only—one of the two reporters, the other being a Frenchman. This occasioned sort of requests from both Reuters and UPI, who were competing with the AP, for me to help them out. I didn't have any particular, you know, strong relationship with the AP, they would pay me for whatever I sent. And I felt at the time, "You know, I need the money," and so I made an arrangement with Reuters and UPI that if something came up, I would file for AP first. Then I would file for Reuters, a little more. And then finally, if I had the time, I'd send something for UPI. But I felt, you know, that my loyalty was primarily with the AP, they'll get the first break. They'll get 10 minutes to use the story. And so, I remember on one occasion, when Prince Souphanouvong, who was then the communist leader, later, by the late '70s, he became president of Laos, because the Pathet Lao ultimately won the Laotian war. But he escaped from prison. And early hours of the morning, when I learned about it, I filed two or three paragraphs for the AP: "Urgent: Souphanouvong Escapes." Big beat. Then I filed a little more detailed for Reuters, but, you know, later in the morning, and then finally, for UPI, I sent a little more. So, next day, I got three messages back at my headquarters at the, at the Constellation Hotel, which was where the reporters would hang out when they came to town. And the first was from the AP, which is, "Thanks, you [were] 10 minutes [ahead] of Reuters, congratulations." And Reuters messaged me, "You were late on breaking development, but ultimately made up with detail," and the third from UPI said, "Thanks for helping out." [Laughs] So, I never did that again. But it was—I was sort of taking care of everyone. Of course, when I joined The Associated Press the next year, my loyalty was totally...

KOMOR: Was totally...

ARNETT: To the organization.

KOMOR: And when did you arrive in Saigon? Do you remember the day?

ARNETT: I flew to Saigon on June 26, 1962, on what I presumed would be a temporary assignment. At that point, Vietnam was a very small-bore involvement for the United States. When I got there, there [were] maybe 5,000 military advisers, spending maybe a million dollars a day. But in different countries around the world, in 40 or 50 other countries, there were American advisers, as many as 500 or a thousand, helping friendly governments organize their armed forces. And the Kennedy administration was still very concerned about Laos. In fact, there was a—Averell

Harriman, then a special ambassador for the Kennedy administration, had gone to Geneva and organized a deal with the Laotian authorities, the three ruling factions, that basically neutralized Laos, and allowed a coalition, sort of left-wing government to take over. By moving Laos out of the way with this political solution, the US Government was clear to concentrate all its efforts on saving South Vietnam from communism. And this didn't happen until, say, mid-'62, so Vietnam was still on the back burner. So, I went to Vietnam presuming to be a temporary assignment. I had visited Vietnam earlier, as a tourist, in 1957, when I'd first got to Southeast Asia with my then-girlfriend Myrtle. And after the pleasures and fun in Thailand, and in Cambodia, where you had Buddhist people, you know, seemingly easygoing and pleasant, going into Vietnam was, it was then a war zone. The French had been fighting there for a decade; there was barbwire everywhere; there were, there were block houses with troops. And the population of Saigon in the marketplaces and around the hotels seemed very negative and difficult. With good reason at that point, they'd been sort of involved in conflict, you know, since the 1930s—occupied by the Japanese, reoccupied by the French, you know, fighting the French. So when I was asked to go back there in '62 I figured, "Ahh. It's sort of an imposition." But, if the AP wanted it, I would do it, but I much preferred the more friendly climes of, you know, Bangkok or Cambodia or Singapore, or even Indonesia. There was also the issue of Malcolm Browne, who at that point, as far as the AP people in the region were concerned, was something of a intellectual bore. Why? Mal was like Ivy League, from Swarthmore College, with a degree in chemistry. And no one else in the AP—none of the Americans in the AP had been to a school like that; most of them, if they'd gone to college, were from the Midwest. I hadn't been to college; I'd come right out of high school into the news business. And Mal was somehow distant with people who had visited; he sort of kept his own counsel. He was this tall, six-foot-three blond, sort of, detached attitude. And he wrote very long pieces for the AP. Thousands of words—two or three thousand words long about his adventures going out with Vietnamese troops, going to the highlands. And to the disgust of many AP people in the region, they would run on the wire. Why did they run? Because Wes, who was taking over as president at that point, adored Mal; figured out that, you know, he was adding immensely to, you know, the value of the AP report by writing these pieces, and fully supported him. But the regular AP guys are saying, "What's a 3,000-word story doing on the wire?" So, for all those reasons, I felt that, you know, life with Mal may not be easy, because he was so very different from other AP people I'd worked for.

KOMOR: Do you—was Mal more or less on his own by the—when you arrived? Was it a—or was Horst [Faas] already there?

ARNETT: Now, when I arrived—I arrived in Saigon from, from Bangkok. The same day Horst arrived, but he came in from Laos. So, we missed each other at the airport, but we ended up in, in the Caravelle Hotel together. I had not met Horst prior to that time. He had taken over from the, the AP photographer for the region, Fred Waters, who was a beloved figure, you know, a pleasant drunk who took an occasional picture, but, one of the boys; one of the holdovers from World War II and Korea. As were most of the AP staff out there at the time. But Mal Browne represented something new, Ivy League, intellectual.

KOMOR: Right.

ARNETT: A bore. A man who is not prone to go drinking with the boys very much.

KOMOR: Did you like Mal?

ARNETT: So, all I had heard was the scuttlebutt, that somehow Mal was a downer. And this was something like, the new AP, and, particularly from a man like Fred Waters, the AP photographer who had been in Saigon but whose job was now lost because Horst was brought in, you know, and Horst was brought in because of his energetic coverage of Africa and Germany, and he's a very brave, bold, smart man. So, the old guard was starting to shift, and Horst and Mal represented that. And I was sort of an appendage, brought along. I got on immediately with Mal, because I enjoyed his, his intellect. You know. He didn't talk about drinking and girls all the time; rarely of the time. He was into the story. He gave me fascinating documents and books to read about the Viet Cong and the, the history of the war. You know, he was very productive; wrote superb analyses. And allowed me to go and do what I felt I needed to do. Now, he would give me guidance; in fact, he did the wonderful, the wonderful, how would you call it? The wonderful memo that he wrote, the, the— what we call...

KOMOR: Well, the, the bureau manual.

ARNETT: OK. He wrote the wonderful bureau manual, basically for me. He wrote it before I got there. Because he figured at that point in time, June of '62, that the war was starting to build up to a degree that most journalists didn't understand. So Mal put together that bureau manual, to prepare. And this was Mal. So I got into the bureau; he said, "Hello." We chatted a little; he gave me the bureau manual and says, "Go and read that, and see you tomorrow." And the bureau manual was wonderful, it gave advice about what cocktail parties to go in, in Saigon; who to believe in the embassy; what parts of the cities to go for different things. And then, of course, the battlefield; how to conduct yourself under fire. One wonderful example was he said, "If you're in a paddy field, crawling through the grass with the troops, and you hear gunfire, don't put your head up to see where it's coming from, because you'll be the next target." Wonderful stuff like that. That was Mal, I, I mean, who else in the AP would have ever bothered doing that kind of manual at that time? So, I read the manual, and I found that Mal encouraged me to do enterprise reporting; to travel to the highlands and around the place. He—we shared responsibility for the daily news product, you know, covering the obvious events that had to be covered; the press conferences, the visits, the battles. But we fared, and within a few months, I think we were part of a wonderful team. I mean, he didn't argue with me; I didn't argue with him. And I really understood that he was, you know, he was—he was doing the kind of journalism that I hadn't realized existed. Demanding accountability of the local officials and government. You know, the intellectual capability he showed in researching, you know, what— not just what motivated the enemy, but weapons used. You know, he had, he had important skills that made his, you know, his stories come alive. That's why they were being used on the AP, not just because Wes Gallagher favored him. And I picked up on that, you know, from the beginning. Because I really—I was like a sponge, sucking in all this information. New Zealand, and Australian, and Thailand journalism; provincial, cautious, noncontroversial. But here was Mal Browne, who had covered the civil rights movement in the South as a young reporter; who'd covered the Bay of Pigs and had been to Cuba, coming to Vietnam and saying, you know, "The ambassador, the generals have to be accountable." At the press conference he'd ask difficult questions. You know. He would write stories [laughs], you know, pointing out the discrepancies in the official picture. And he would—and he had a great writing style. So I really modeled myself on Mal. And— for the next four years, because he did stay in—running the bureau until 1965. And to this day, he remains a great pal. In fact, I try to see him whenever I can, but I, you know, still respect him enormously. And he's had a great career, of course, later with *The New York Times*. But that was my beginning. Now, in addition, I was so fortunate to be part of an influx of very bright young American journalists. David Halberstam came a few weeks after I was there; he moved in, working out of the Saigon AP bureau. One reason, because *The New York Times* usually worked out of AP, because of the close relationship, and secondly because he had a personal relationship with Horst Faas from coverage in the Congo, the previous year. So he knew Horst very well; in fact, they got a house together; shared the house. And also, there was Stanley Karnow, who became, you know, the great historian of the Vietnam War, but who worked for Time magazine. He was a frequent visitor out of Hong Kong. And Neil Sheehan, who was then a young UPI reporter, who would hang around, and there was just a handful of us. We'd have coffee together. There was no big partying there; there was no big drinking. You know, we weren't—this was a different sort of crowd. You know, they, they were just enjoying being part of what they figured was a very significant story, and it became significant very quickly, with a series of major battles in the country-side, where the Viet Cong emerged as a, quite a formidable force, plus the deterioration of the ability of the president of Vietnam, Ngo Dinh Diem, to maintain control. And you had a rising Viet Cong movement, guerrilla movement, then you had an angry Buddhist movement that, that opposed this Catholic dictator, Ngo Dinh Diem. And the story quickly morphed into, you know, the most significant one in U.S. foreign policy, and remained that way, really, for the next decade. So I was sort of cushioned by this group of brilliant young journalists. And I learned from them; I'm a quick study. [Laughs] But I learned from them, and I really admired them, and to this day they remain

181

friends of mine. Halberstam, Sheehan and Karnow, you know, I really, I was so lucky to fall into the hands of such bright people. Because our lives are shaped by our mentors and my mentors happened to be journalists my own age. And I quickly learned to believe in what they believed in, you know, information; the truth of it; the worth of taking a risk—the importance of taking risks for information, to tell the truth. And this attitude pervaded a successive wave of reporters coming to Vietnam. In the AP, you had a whole group of—John Wheeler came a few years into the war, and then Richard Pyle, and so many others, that I could go through a whole list.

KOMOR: Tell me, tell me about your relationship with George Esper. Because he feels, I think, to this day that you were his mentor, in a way. And so, and so one returns the favor, as you go along, in mentoring people, in return for those mentors that you were lucky to have. What was George like? When did he come over?

ARNETT: George came to Vietnam in 1965. A West Virginia boy; his father, family had worked in the coal mines. But he was the child who made it through college. Various small AP bureaus; volunteered for Saigon, and he was sent there in mid-1965. I mean, he initially, you know, initially became friendly to me because I gave him what he felt was, you know, significant advice. I remember visiting him in his hotel room, soon after he arrived, and he had been out on a trip with, on a patrol with the, with the Vietnamese troops. He had come back, and he was full of himself, and I went into the bathroom to use the toilet, and I noticed his muddy boots were in the bidet. And I said—and I came out, and he said, "You know, Peter, these, these French, they even have a special appliance to wash your damn boots." I pointed out to George that a bidet was for more than just washing boots. [Laughs] But he felt—from then on in, he looked to me for advice about, you know, modern living. [Laughs] The—you know, George was, you know, one of the truly dedicated, you know, AP people, who came to Vietnam. Well, in a way, I feel sort of similar to him, in which that, you know, I felt that you take a story and you, you know, you shake it like a dog shakes a bone, you know, you're not going to let it go. And George had that similar feel to a story. He just wanted to grip it. And with George, it was a matter of just leading him in the right direction. And say, "George, you know, we need you in Danang; the Marines are going to do this." So George would be up to Danang, and you would get everything you ever wanted to know about what the Marines were doing in that operation. Not only would you get whatever you needed to know, but you would get it in a competitive period, he was the most competitive journalist I'd ever seen, and he would compete with UPI and everyone else, you know? And he diligently, fervently, believed that the most important role he had in life was to serve the requirements of the AP, which was to serve—to get the story. George is actually still like that, if you—now he's in retirement, but if you give him, you know, a suggestion that maybe he should look someone up, or maybe he should—he'll grab it and do it fervently. But, you know, for a wire service like the AP, who, who needed diligence, and who, you know, needed industry and competitiveness, George was the man. In addition, he was the most decent of people, until you crossed him. And there's one famous story of George. He was dictating from Danang late in 1965, at the newly opened press center, notable because there was only one telephone line from Danang to Saigon, which was one more than from Saigon to the headquarters in New York; there were no telephone lines. You could rarely call. And this one telephone line from Danang to Saigon was used often by all the media, because by late '65, with the first of, the first 100,000 of half a million U.S. troops having come in, there was a lot of people wanting to use the phone, particularly UPI, and television networks. So I remember George was dictating a story to me about some press conference the Marines had just had, and I heard someone, some noise in the background, and George said, "Excuse me." And I heard more noise, and a thump. And then he got back on the phone, and I said, "What was that?" "Oh, nothing." We later learned that an ABC correspondent had tried to take the phone away from George, telling him that he'd been on it for an hour, and that was too long, so George, you know, decked him right there on the spot. [Laughs] And went back to the phone. Without, you know, missing a beat. "Nothing, Peter, nothing. Just continue." But his generosity of spirit, I mean, impressed all. He was a beloved figure, but a very competitive figure. And there are the stories of legion about, you know how—I remember one particular story in '67, when we heard from a White House source that President Johnson was going to visit Cam Ranh Bay. Now, you could imagine that security was very strict when the president went anywhere, particularly a place like Vietnam. It's like when President Bush made his one visit to Iraq, no one knew about it until he was well gone. So, Johnson was on his way to Cam Ranh Bay. We got a tip. But not even the White House press corps knew that he was going. But, so, George figured, you know, "We're going to get this story first." So we called up the Cam Ranh Bay airport, and got the airport duty officer and said, "General Esper here. Is the president there yet?" "Well, sir, his plane is just coming in." "Well, stay on the line! I want to know if everything's all right. Give me a report on what's happening." So, this officer, who was standing, you know, overlooking them, "Well, President Johnson's arrived. He's being greeted by General So-and-So, and there's a, there's an honor guard and, you know, and the president's shaking hands, and moving around, and he did this, and he huddled with someone, and he met President Thieu, and"—"Well, thank you, Colonel." So—but he still kept him on the line, while busily typing, and then as the colonel said, "Well, the plane's just taking off," it was a, you know, like 25-minute visit; George had the story prepared, boom. Instantly. [Laughs] President Johnson. That is George! Of course, the AP White House people were very disconcerted and unhappy that when they got back to Thailand, they'd been scooped. With all the details. [Laughs]

KOMOR: And I seem to remember that he got him to read the text of his remarks over the phone.

ARNETT: I believe that was even the case. A text of his remarks over the phone.

KOMOR: Yes.

ARNETT: That had been given in advance.

KOMOR: Yes. I guess you have to have—"Would you like to hear?" Because he—yeah.

ARNETT: Yeah! "Would you like to hear, by the way, what he said?" [Laughs]

KOMOR: [Laughs] Yeah.

ARNETT: Well, you know the story—it was just a marvelous, but this is—"General Esper here."

KOMOR: Yes.

ARNETT: So, he could do that. George, who seems at time passively—responsive—unresponsive—actually has a lot going on in his brain, and he could write really dramatically, and good stories. The—you know, George spent more time in the bureau than out, because he was such a diligent editor and writer that he would use that phone, you know, better than anyone else I had ever seen. I remember, there was a story that came out of Washington of a B-52 pilot who had refused to fly. And he had been grounded. In, in, in Thailand, at one of the—Udorn, Thailand, one of the B-52 bases. George got him on the phone. Again by saying, "General Esper here," you know, and he got the guy on the phone. And got an exclusive from, [laughs] from this pilot that had been put into solitary, but they'd given him a call from General Esper, you know, to reprimand him. And George got the whole story. But he was capable of doing that. And there was constantly many, many stories of George's ability. But by staying in the bureau, you know, this, this meant that he, he became secondary to the field correspondents. You know, so I'd be out covering the war, and getting great stories, and George would be back in the office, helping, doing the overnight report. Now, George being such a decent man, filled with humility, never challenged that. He never demanded to go out on the story, to get—for a change. He was willing to put up with all that. So that's why, at the end of the war, it was such a great pleasure for me to be in Saigon. For many reasons, I wanted to be in Saigon in April of '75, when the Vietnam War came to an end; when the communists ultimately struck down through the many South Vietnamese provinces to encircle Saigon and then pounce, come in, with all the U.S. forces leaving. Excuse me. So, I was sent in to help the coverage in the last weeks. George Esper was there, Ed White, and Matt Franjola, who was a stringer who had come in. And as the, as the crisis neared it, its, you know, the completion of the war, AP ordered most people out. But they let George and I and Franjola stay. And when it became clear that the communists were coming in, George said to me, "Peter, you know, you're the senior man here; you're the best; you do the big story." And I said, "George, no. You've sat at that desk, you know, for 10 years. You've put your name on every overnight story, and no one knows who you are. You write the story." Next day, headline of *The New York Times*, front page: "Saigon Falls," by George Esper. It was one of the great moments, you know, in any headline collection. "Saigon Falls," by George Esper. So, it was so—I was so happy to see that all those years on the desk brought— which was a fabulous headline. I mean, that's through history now. And it's George Esper on that story. Now, George is inordinately grateful to me; he keeps saying that, that, and publicly, that "It was Peter Arnett; he should have got a Pulitzer for the fall of Saigon." Rubbish! I got my Pulitzer years earlier. George deserved a Pulitzer, actually, for his excellent reporting, he did. In addition to doing the roundup, he did superb eyewitness accounts of suicides and so much else. But he still gives me credit. But that's George, you know? He, he, he is so, you know, so willing, so humble. He's got so much humility.

KOMOR: I want to ask you a fairly—a big question, on a huge topic, but we haven't discussed too much the nitty-gritty of coverage of Vietnam. But, in hindsight, I wonder if you have any observations about the Vietnam coverage as a whole, and how it was handled. And perhaps how has, how have you seen war coverage change since Vietnam? And obviously, it's a humongous topic.

ARNETT: The AP Vietnam coverage; the American media Vietnam coverage was distinctive in a special way. This was the first war, the first modern war—and I include all of the wars of the 20th century as being modern wars—where the media held government, government officials, and military officers, and military officials, accountable for their decisions. World War I, World War II, Korea: strict censorship, limited commentary, limited factual transmission of information by the media. They went along with it, because those three wars, World War I, II and Korea, were looked upon as wars of national security; the fate of the nation was involved in those wars. There needed to be, you know, a national effort, and that included censorship of the media, which under the Constitution or, in the eons of time since the Constitution had been written, came to understand that in special occasions you can censor the press. So, reporters in those three wars essentially were part of the military. They got military rank; officers, depending on the place within the news media the reporter occupied, would be a senior officer or a junior officer. And they marched to the media's—to the military's drummer. The stories were censored; there was self-censorship; that was understood. And in fact, this was seen as a necessary ingredient of previous coverage. I remember John Steinbeck wrote a book called, you know,

PETER ARNETT: AN ORAL HISTORY

The War That Was, or words to that effect.* And in it, there was a preface that I actually read soon after I got to Vietnam, in which he said, "The war the media wrote about, World War II, was not the real war. The real war ended up, you know, in the editor's waste-paper basket." And he, he explained why that was, and he also suggested it was probably necessary to do it, but the point is, so much of the brutality and the stupidity of these wars, the earlier wars, was not reported. Because it was deemed of national security, and you just could not shake resolve, and anything negative, too negative, could hurt opinion back home. It was seen, argued by the authorities, and they got away with it; the media went along with it. Let's go to Vietnam. The primary reporters of the Vietnam War, and I'm talking about Halberstam of the *Times*, and those who followed him at the *Times*; Malcolm Browne at the AP, and those who followed him; *Time* magazine; *Newsweek*. These were reporters who came up during the civil rights struggle in the '50s. Quite a few of them had been covering the South. They'd also all been in the military. Because I'd served two years in the military, all reporters, at that time, was com-pulsory military service. So, they were all very familiar with the military; had their own feelings about the military that weren't very patriotic, because certainly the military in the late '50s, you know, service had

---

* *Once There Was a War* (1958).

become very routine. You know, as the young people in the United States were you know, moving out in their own directions—the civil rights struggle; other issues had come to the fore; women's rights. There was a, sort of a fervent, you know, desire by young Americans to bring change. This was evident in the young reporters. They're the ones who came to Vietnam in the '60s. And with that attitude, they immediately began challenging government. So that when I got to Vietnam in '62, Malcolm Browne was writing stories saying, you know, "The U.S. Embassy is lying because they're bringing in helicopters and tanks to help the South Vietnamese and saying it's not so." So David Halberstam would come in, and go to the Mekong Delta, and saying, "You know, all the American advisers that I talk to say that we're losing the war there. The Vietnam—Viet Cong are growing in ability, you know, they have controls." And me, being an observant young reporter, picked up on all that. This made Vietnam different: challenging authority, challenging the embassy, challenging the government. So, by the, by 1963, President Kennedy was demanding *The New York Times* pull David Halberstam out of Vietnam, because he didn't like his coverage. He said, "Halberstam is too negative," particularly writing about the Buddhist crisis, and its impact on the presidency of Ngo Dinh Diem. In 1965, President Lyndon Johnson, you know, was calling on the AP to pull me out of Vietnam because my reports were seen as being negative and what made it worse, I was from New Zealand. Of course, New Zealand was an ally; it had, you know, four or five thousand troops in Vietnam [laughs], but that wasn't the issue. Every day on the ticker, on his—in the teleprinter in the Oval Office, you know, Johnson would read these AP dispatches, and every now and again they had a Peter Arnett story, or a John Wheeler story, and others that challenged the conventional wisdom, and that made him, made him very unhappy. But not just the AP and *The New York Times*. *Newsweek*, *Time* magazine started to, you know, to look at this war as being, you know, misspent money, misspent lives. This hadn't happened before. This was also unique. And the ability, then, of journalists to analyze and challenge government in what was, you know, a war seen to be the wrong war in the wrong place at the wrong time carried over into the '70s, with Watergate, where *Washington Post* reporters felt emboldened to challenge authority right at home. [Bob] Woodward and [Carl] Bernstein challenged the authority of the president in Washington. Not without difficulty; they had to convince their own editors that what they were doing was significant. Now, the effect of Watergate, and the effect of Vietnam coverage, carried over into the '80s, with strong critical coverage of Americans' involvement in Central America; with the Iran-Contra affair, supporting the Contras against the Nicaraguan government; going on to the first Gulf War; and then going on to the '90s; and it was only, really, 9/11 that changed the picture, where journalists and where mainstream media—people, reporters, editors, you know, felt confronted by terrorism, that altered the picture to some degree. But those years from the early '60s to early in the 21st century were really years of challenging, significant, important journalism that, that helped really disclose what government was doing abroad; the mistakes it was making, and, you know, and bringing the public into a greater understanding and a greater role to play in how government acted abroad. There's no doubt about it.

KOMOR: Do you see that AP had a specific role to play in that—fulfilling that great journalistic ideal? Was it, did it operate differently from other news organizations? And how is it different?

ARNETT: The AP in the 1960s and '70s was basically as it is today: the rock of coverage. I mean, today, all American mainstream news organizations look to the AP wire for guidance; for the latest news. Now, maybe they'll look at CNN, if they want a press coverage live, and a—if, they'll look at the other 24-hour networks if there's a big developing story, if there's a Katrina.* But basically, day in and day out, the AP wire is the

---

* Hurricane Katrina (2005).

guidepost; the example. The unchallenged, you know, truth, as best being determined, of what's going on. And this was the case in the 1960s. It also applied to the AP during the previous wars. Don't forget the AP operated under censorship. It didn't challenge censorship because it was understood that in wars of national security, you have censorship. But bearing that in mind, they would push the censor, you know, to get more information into the report, but there was an understanding. You're censored? OK, we understand that, but let's try and get a little more on the wire than you would normally get. Like, when I was in Baghdad for CNN in the first Gulf War, I was the only reporter there. So, the Iraqis would say, you know, "You're allowed two minutes a day to report and we want to censor what you write." "OK, so this is what I'm going to write, but you know, I have to get on the air, and I have to talk about a few other things." "OK." So you keep expanding the perimeter, as best you can. And that's what the AP did in World War II and World War I. The important thing though, is to admit that you're under censorship. So, when I was in the Gulf War, every report I did, CNN said "under censorship." And in World War II and World War I, it was understood by the public and everyone that there was censorship in place. There was a general in charge of censorship. There was never any pretense that there wasn't censorship. You know. It was a requirement that news organizations remembered, that as Walter Cronkite has said, "You still had the reporter's presence with the 101st Airborne when they leaped in at, you know, D-Day, you know, June 5, 1944." Cronkite was with them. So their report was censored, but the point is, he was there, he had his notes; sooner or later, you could write your book, or give the bigger picture. It's simply the information you had was, you know, significant, you know, you had to be a time delay on it. So, there was no pretense. We knew they had—you had censorship. In Vietnam, there was no time delay. There was no censorship. Why wasn't there any censorship? Well, the succession of U.S. governments: the Kennedy administration; the Johnson administration; the Nixon administration, refused to admit there was a war on. It was sort of a police action. It was an insurgency. It was never officially perceived as being a war. And Secretary of State Dean Rusk mentioned after the war, when asked why hadn't censorship been imposed, he said, "Well, we didn't want to bring the focus of the war up to the level where if we—the imposition of censorship would have brought into place so many other requirements. You introduce censorship, you introduce mobilization, and you have to bring so much else into play when you have censorship in this democracy." They didn't want to do that. They didn't quite know what they were doing in

Vietnam. There was no plan to win the war, so they had to live with a media that challenged what they were doing. And the media was basically saying, you know, "Get out of here!" You know, that, that, that was climaxed after the Tet Offensive in February of 1968, when Walter Cronkite had come back from a tour of the war zone, and on CBS said, you know, "We're losing this. What are we doing there? It's not working." And Walter Cronkite was a voice that was more respected than Lyndon Johnson's at the time, so Johnson just declined to run for office again. [Laughs] It was—so this was—what the AP brought then, was, and the other media, was an insistence that, you know, the facts should not be concealed. If the government felt it was such a big issue, go ahead and, go ahead and impose censorship. Don't ask us for self-censorship. The worst censorship is self-censorship. It's like me going to—in Iraq, and seeing a beheading, or seeing some terrible action, and not talking about. Particularly, it was done by American troops. It's concealing the Abu Ghraib pictures, because it's not in the national interest to do it. It's not our job to do that. If the Pentagon wants to impose censorship, do it, but with the understanding that, you know, that the nation trusts your best judgment. And it, it's—and will hold you accountable. If the media is asked to self-censorship, who's accountable? You know, this is not good. And throughout the Vietnam War, Wes Gallagher was unwilling to impose self-censorship. He was unwilling to tell us, "Well, guys, go to the field, but don't report any atrocities you might see committed by Americans." You know? You know, "Let's not—let's have a more optimistic assessment of where we are in 1967." You had President—you know, you had Lyn—you—General William C. Westmoreland, then the commander in Vietnam in November of 1967, came, told Congress, "We're winning the war; there's a light at the end of the tunnel." Did Wes Gallagher say, "Hey, why don't you do something that supports that?" No! He said, "Is that right or wrong?" I did a piece which said it was wrong. You know? So. But he didn't—what he challenged, what he demanded of the AP staff was that you had to be correct. And I saw Wes a few times; I'd come back to the States; he would come to Vietnam, and he'd say, "Peter, you're a great reporter. Don't ever be wrong. You're so—there's so many people who don't like what you're doing that if you were wrong we won't be able to do anything to hold you." I didn't do anything wrong. [Laughs] So. Not in Vietnam anyway. And so, it was. That was the attitude. "We'll go with the reporters; they're risking their lives. We'll go with what they're reporting to us. And this is how it has to be in a democratic society." And I think this was an incredibly important standard that the AP certainly helped—or led. The AP led the reporting. I mean, we had the more reporters; more photographers; we were first with the story more often than UPI; we—the analyses we did held up, still hold up. You know, we gave 4 dead, 18 wounded to the story, and we're willing to do that. And this was a wonderful commitment. And, and it was, and, it, it was a necessary commitment, you know, and it was, and something that we can all be proud of. I'm proud of it; Richard Pyle's proud; Esper is proud. Every AP reporter who served in Vietnam, that was their proudest time of their career. With good reason! Because we really believed in, you know, our requirement to tell the truth of what's going on; demand accountability; get to the bottom of what's happening. And don't forget, the Vietnam War was over a course of time; it was from, basically, '62 to '75. It was a long time, a lot of challenging—it was a challenging time. It's sort of like Iraq today; it's very challenging. And Vietnam was challenging, but I think from beginning to end, I think the media held up pretty well. And historians have agreed with that assessment. There are those on the right side of the spectrum who blame the press for losing the war. But even military historians, in their volumes they've written about the media, conclude that we were on top of it all. If there's any challenge, it's the fact that information came out that shouldn't have. But that's not up to us to determine.

It's up to the authorities to, you know, to either not do those things, or have kind of controls that the public is aware of, that we're aware of, but which require accountability eventually.

KOMOR: Thank you, Peter.

ARNETT: My pleasure.

Compiled by Sarit Hand, Coordinator, The Associated Press Oral History Program, AP Corporate Archives, Oct. 8, 2009.

ORIGINAL SOURCES

from the AP Corporate Archives

[*transcription begins on page 205*]

```
U
FYMEON
I167
    E
  VIETNAM DIARY
  SAIGON (AP)—TUESDAY, APRIL 29.
  4:00 A.M.-- THE DAY BEGINS EARLY, THE THUMPING OF ROCKETS
AT SAIGON'S TAN SON NHUT AIR BASE. IT IS A REPLAY OF1968
WHEN THE COMMUNIST COMMAND'S TET OFFENSIVE SIMILARLY OBLITERATED
PART OF THE CITY AND THE BEST VANTAGE POINT IN TOWN WAS AGAIN
THE CARAVELLE HOTEL WHERE IN THE PRE-DAWN HOURS NEWSMEN AGAIN
COUNTED THE ROCKETS EXPLODING WITH BRIGHT BALLS OF FIRE.
THERE IS A NEW TWIST THIS TIME, BRILLIANTLY YELLOW PATH BURNED
BY THE STRELA MISSILE, A HAND- FIRED SOVIET-BUILT WEAPON THAT
DOWNED THREE AIRCRAFT IN FULL VIEW OF THE NEWSMEN.


      ---


  8:45 A.M.-- THEY'RE PULLING THE PLUG. THE U.S. EMBASSY HAS
QUIETLY PASSED THE WORD THAT ALL AMERICANS WILL LEAVE TODAY ENDING
30 YEARS OF AMERICAN INVOLVEMENT IN VIETNAM. THE EMBASSY STAFF
AND THE FEW MILITARY PEOPLE LEFT HAD NO CHOICE. THEY HAD TO GO.
NEWSMEN DID HAVE THE CHOICE AND A HANDFUL REMAINED TO SEE THE
LAST FEW HOURS OF THE COUNTRY THAT HAD FLOWERED JUST BRIEFLY
ON THE INTERNATIONAL SCENE.
                  MORE
                  ARNETT/ESPER
    TAN-2230ST
```

The "Vietnam Diary" dispatches from Peter Arnett and George Esper (page 1 of 3), sent as the city of Saigon fell to the North Vietnamese on Tuesday, Apr. 29, 1975. Original wire copy.
(AP Corporate Archives)

```
I168

    R

   SAIGON--VIETNAM DIARY  2

    NOON--THE MAD EVACUATION SCRAMBLE STARTS. ASSOCIATED PRESS
PHOTOGRAPHER NEAL ULEVICH HAD TO BE SUMMONED FROM THE POST AND
TELEGRAPH OFFICE WHERE HE WAS SENDING RADIOPHOTOS OF THE ROCKETING
OF THE AIRPORT. HE DID NOT HAVE TIME TO CHECK OUT OF HIS HOTEL ROOM
AND LEFT WITH ONLY HIS CAMERAS. ANOTHER AP STAFFER, CARL
ROBINSON, BARELY HAD TIME TO LOCATE HIS NEWLY ADOPTED  VIETNAMESE
DAUGHTER.  OLD INDOCHINA HAND ED WHITE, WHO HAS COVERED VIETNAM
FOR THE AP OFF AND ON SINCE 1962, CRAMMED HIMSELF INTO A CROWDED
BUS AND SAID, "THIS IS NOT THE WAY I WANTED TO LEAVE INDOCHINA."


    ---
    ...

    4:00 P.M.-- THIS WAS THE LAST CHANCE FOR THOSE VIETNAMESE WHO
WANTED TO GO TO GO. RUMORS HAD IT THE VIET CONG WOULD BE IN
THE CITY BY MORNING. STREETS AROUND THE U.S. EMBASSY BECAME
CLOGGED WITH THE LAST DESPERATE VIETNAMESE TRYING FOR A NEW
LIFE IN THE UNITED STATES AS AGAINST THE REGIMENTED LIFE THEY
HAD BEEN LED TO EXPECT UNDER COMMUNISM.

    ---
    ...

        MORE
    TAN-223 7ST
```

The "Vietnam Diary" dispatches from Peter Arnett and George Esper (page 2 of 3), sent as the city of Saigon fell to the North Vietnamese on Tuesday, Apr. 29, 1975. Original wire copy.
(AP Corporate Archives)

R

SAIGON--VIETNAM DIARY 3

IN THE HASTE TO LEAVE WHAT WAS VALUABLE YESTERDAY WAS WORTHLESS
TODAY. THE OWNER OF A LOCAL AMERICAN RESTAURANT GAVE AP REPORTER
MATT FRANJOLA, WHO STAYED ON, HIS JEEP. ANOTHER AP REPORTER WHO
STAYED, PETER ARNETT, WAS PRESENTED WITH A DIPLOMATIC LICENSED
CAR BY A DEPARTING JAPANESE FRIEND. NEWSMEN WHO HAD DEPARTED
WITHOUT TIME TO PAY THEIR HOTEL BILLS OFFERED THOSE STAYING
BEHIND ALL THE POSSESSIONS IN THE ROOMS IF THEY WOULD PAY THE RENT.

NIGHTFALL: THE WORST FEARS START TO BE REALIZED. SHOOTING
BREAKS OUT IN THE STREETS AROUND THE AP OFFICE IN DOWNTOWN SAIGON
AS DRUNKEN SOLDIERS SHOOT OFF THEIR WEAPONS. SUDDENLY ALL POWER
IS CUT. COMMUNICATIONS WITH OUR NEW YORK OFFICE ARE BROKEN.
IT IS RAINING HEAVILY OUTSIDE. YOU CAN'T SEE A THING. ARE THE
VIET CONG IN TOWN ALREADY? ONE WONDERS. DID THEY CUT THE POWER?
THE LIGHTS SOON GO ON AGAIN. THE SOLDIERS GO HOME TO SLEEP
IT OFF. WE FILE OUR NIGHT REPORT AND THE FIRST DAY WITHOUT
THE AMERICANS IS OVER.

ENDIT

ARNETT/ESPER

I   TAM-224 7ST

The "Vietnam Diary" dispatches from Peter Arnett and George Esper (page
3 of 3), sent as the city of Saigon fell to the North Vietnamese on Tuesday, Apr.
29, 1975. Original wire copy.
(AP Corporate Archives)

[Eds: (sic) in a transcription indicates a spelling or grammatical error in the original document]

VIETNAM DIARY

Peter Arnett and George Esper, "Vietnam Diary", Apr. 29, 1975. Wirecopy, Various Wires, Oversize Folder. AP Corporate Archives, New York.

Saigon (AP)—Tuesday, April 29. [1975]

4:00 a.m.—The day begins early, the thumping of rockets at Saigon's Tan Son Nhut air base. It is a replay of 1968 when the communist command's Tet Offensive similarly obliterated part of the city and the best vantage point in town was again the Caravelle Hotel where in the pre-dawn hours newsmen again counted the rockets exploding with bright balls of fire. There is a new twist this time, brilliantly yellow path burned by the Strela missile, a hand-fired Soviet-built weapon that downed three aircraft in full view of the newsmen.

8:45 a.m.—They're pulling the plug. The U.S. Embassy has quietly passed the word that all Americans will leave today ending 30 years of American involvee-ment *(sic)* in Vietnam. The Embassy staff and the few military people left had no choice. They had to go. Newsmen did have the choice and a handful remained to see the last few hours of the country that had flowered just briefly on the international scene.

Noon—The mad evacuation scramble starts. Associated Press photographer Neal Ulevich had to be summoned from the post and telegraph office where he was sending radiophotos of the rocketing of the airport. He did not have time to check out of his hotel room and left with only his cameras. Another AP staffer, Carl Robinson, barely had time to locate his newly adopted Vietnamese daughter. Old Indochina hand Ed White, who has covered Vietnam for the AP off and on since 1962, crammed himself into a crowded bus and said, "This is not the way I wanted to leave Indochina."

4:00 p.m.—This was the last chance for those Vietnamese who wanted to go to go. Rumors had it the Viet Cong would be in the city by morning. Streets around the U.S. Embassy became clogged with the last desperate Vietnamese trying for a new life in the United States as against the regimented life they had been led to expect under communism.

In the haste to leave what was valuable yesterday was worthless today. The owner of a local American restaurant gave AP reporter Matt Franjola, who stayed on, his Jeep. Another AP reporter who stayed, Peter Arnett, was presented with a diplomatic licensed car by a departing Japanese friend. Newsmen who had departed without time to pay their hotel bills offered those staying behind all the possessions in the rooms if they would pay the rent.

Nightfall: the worst fears start to be realized. Shooting breaks out in the streets around the AP office in downtown Saigon as drunken soldiers shoot off their weapons. Suddenly all power is cut. Communications with our New York office are broken. It is raining heavily outside. You can't see a thing. Are the Viet Cong in town already? One wonders. Did they cut the power? The lights soon go on again. The soldiers go home to sleep it off. We file our night report and the first day without the Americans is over.

Endit.

Arnett/Esper

said-

dak to reconstruction   my eyes.

(editors note: the b   the fiercest of the

vietnam war. an associated p   o spent ten days at the

battle scene reconstructs the action   iscusses enemy and

allied tactics.)

by peter arnett

associated press writer

dak to, vietnam, nov. 25 (AP) -- the communists picked the time

and the place for the bloody battle of dak to.

from the time the first enemy shots were fired from a bamboo

thicket at u.s. infantrymen november three, to the painful scramble to

the top of hill 875 by weary u.s. paratroopers on thursday, the

communists made it clear they were at dak to to fight.

it was the nearest thing to a set piece battle yet seen in

the vietnam war. it may still not be over.

yet after 21 days of bloody fighting, allied commanders still

privately confess themselves mystified as to the enemy's real

intentions at dak to.

the initial allied reasoning, that the communists planned to

Peter Arnett's analysis (page 1 of 14) of the battle of Dak To, filed Nov. 25, 1967. Original typescript copy. (AP Corporate Archives)

DAK TO RECONSTRUCTION

Peter Arnett, [Dak To Analysis], Nov. 25, 1967.
Typescript copy, Saigon Bureau Records, Box 36,
Folder 619. AP Corporate Archives, New York.

*(Editor's note: The B[attle of Dak To was one of] the fierc-
est of the Vietnam War. An Associated P[ress correspondent wh]o spent ten days at the battle scene reconstructs
the action [and] discusses enemy and Allied tactics.)*

By Peter Arnett

Associated Press Writer

Dak To, Vietnam, Nov. 25 [1967] (AP) – The communists picked the time and the place for the bloody
battle of Dak To.

From the time the first enemy shots were fired
from a bamboo thicket at U.S. infantrymen on
November three, to the painful scramble to the top of
Hill 875 by weary U.S. paratroopers on Thursday, the
communists made it clear they were at Dak To to fight.

It was the nearest thing to a set piece battle yet
seen in the Vietnam War. It may still not be over.

Yet after 21 days of bloody fighting, Allied commanders still privately confess themselves mystified
as to the enemy's real intentions at Dak To.

The initial Allied reasoning, that the communists planned to [*page 2 missing*]...

[...]The officer was referring to the American casualties taken in capturing the hill, merely one of a thousand knolls that dot the Dak To area. Unofficially, the 173rd airborne brigade took nearly 150 men killed and almost 300 wounded on the hill, at best a one to one ratio with enemy casualties.

Asked if he felt the objective was important, a senior paratrooper officer commented, "Well, it sort of commands the valley, so in a conventional war it would be important. But this isn't a conventional war, so I guess it means nothing."

The nature of the terrain was a major advantage for the communist forces. Each year the enemy's November offensive, launched as the highlands begin drying out from the monsoon, have been steadily shifting north into the jungled hills.

Under the shelter of the triple canopied jungles, the communists can busily build extensive bunkers and trench systems, forcing American troops to rout them out one by one in the worst possible terrain.

The communists must have been working over the Dak To hills for at least three months, and possibly longer, senior American officers believe. The bunker systems stretch across numerous hills, some having caverns with woven bamboo walls and elevated log floors.

One or two turns were in each entrance to seal out napalm, considered the ideal anti-bunker weapon until the Dak To battle. Now it has been shown that in the end, only hand to hand fighting can rout an enemy who digs deep enough.

Twenty or thirty men at the most would conceal themselves in the bunkers. The main ground fighting would be done by flanking forces who would melt into the jungle after the initial infantry clash, leaving those in the bunkers to fight to the end. This accounted for the few bodies found in the bunker systems at the end of the fights.

Each hill top bunker system around Dak To probably took two weeks to construct, U.S. engineers figured, and they were built to withstand the severest Allied bomb onslaught.

From the nature of the hill top emplacements and their number, American intelligence officers believe that the North Vietnamese intended to stand and fight in the lonely Dak To hills and had laid the groundwork well. The enemy has used the Dak To region freely since 1964 when the first North Vietnamese infantry regiments were clandestinely slipped into the south. The district town of Tou Morong and the special forces camp of Dak Sut, both to Dak To's north, were wiped out in 1965.

Two enemy regiments—the 174th and the 24th— were known to be somewhere in the hills, and the U.S.

Army's 173rd airborne brigade chased after them during July, August and September this year. The paratroopers left Dak To early October, confident they would not need to return.

In November the 173rd brigade has been the most severely punished of the three American brigades in the Dak To fight.

American intelligence keeps a close watch on enemy troop activity, but is limited by the scarcity of population in the hills. Two enemy regiments—the 32nd and the 66th—dissappeared (*sic*) from the Cambodian border opposite Pleiku mid-1967 and the search went out for them.

Airforce (*sic*) planes using infrared cameras, helicopters carrying "people sniffers", and long range infantry patrols searched far and wide. The new locale of the lost regiments was eventually determined—the tangled hills around Dak To.

Enemy pressure on the Montagnard villages near Dak To mounted. Special forces patrols reported seeing communist troops entering the Dak To bowl.

The U.S. Fourth Division, commanded by Maj. General William R. Peers, began to move. For months Peers had been waiting for a sign that the communists wanted to fight. He had it now.

The battle of Dak To was on.

The battle has been fought in two parts.

The first part was between November three and November twelve and saw clashes between two American infantry brigades (the 173rd and the First Brigade, 4th Division) and the North Vietnamese 32nd and 66th regiments.

An indication of the battles to come was a tough fight November six when a 173rd company lost 26 killed and 37 wounded on a ridge southwest of Dak To. A total of 84 enemy dead were reported in that battle.

The fight for Hill 724, the first of the Hill fights, took place November eight. Two Fourth Division infantry companies lost ten killed and 47 wounded in that battle.

By November 12 American forces had lost 96 men killed and 498 wounded as against 635 enemy reported dead, and the battle was considered over by the senior American commanders.

The second and bloodiest stage began five days later.

This stage was preceeded (*sic*) by a daring series of mortar attacks on the Dak To airstrip that had become a jucier (*sic*) target each day. Two C-130 transport planes worth nearly three million dollars each were destroyed. An ammo dump with 1,200 tons in it blew up.

General Peers moved in a brigade of reinforcements from the U.S. Army's First Cavalry Division just to be on the safe side. A task force of two Vietnamese airborne battalions moved up.

Three days later and just a few hours after the enemy was said to have withdrawn back across the Cambodian border, the North Vietnamese 24th and 174th regiments moved into Dak To for the attack. The second stage of the battle had begun.

Hill 1338 was fought over November 17. The Vietnamese task force spent three days conquering Hill 1416 (the numerals indicate the hill heights in meters). Hill 882 was taken November 18. The next day the bitter 110-hour fight for Hill 875 began.

"This is submarine warfare," said Lt. General William B. Rosson, senior U.S. commander in the central highlands, referring to the subterranean nature of the communist positions.

The Allied commanders professed to be satisfied with the heavy contact. "The enemy's only choice is to die or retreat," said Brig. General L.H. Schweiter, commander of the 173rd brigade. This remark came back to haunt Schweiter when he had to leave scores of his own wounded in the jungle for fifty hours under enemy mortar fire on Hill 875 before he could get them out.

The enemy tenacity in the Dak To hills astounded the American soldiers and their commanders. General Peers commented, "The enemy has shown outstanding morale and discipline. He stood his ground."

One paratrooper commented, "They fight like they're all John Waynes, three clips each and making every bullet count."

At all times the enemy did have the choice of die-ing (*sic*) or retreating. In none of the battles was he surrounded. He could have melted away into the inpenetrable (*sic*) jungle at any point.

Why did he stay and fight? Certainly it was not for the nobbly (*sic*) hills of Dak To. These are absolutely lacking in strategic value. The communists seemed bent on staying and fighting to the last man, taking as many Americans as possible with them.

Under these circumstances, the conquering of a hill became less a victory than an engineering process, the methodical destruction of the bunkered hill tops with endless air strikes and artillery barrages.

This proved eventually effective on all the hills with the exception of 875 where a U.S. paratroop battalion was pinned down with numerous dead and wounded, unable to overrun the enemy positions and unable to evacuate its wounded.

By Thanksgiving Day the stubborn Hill 875 was taken and the second phase of the Dak To battle appeared over. The latest casualty count is 285 U.S. dead, 18 missing presumed dead, and 988 wounded. Enemy dead was placed at 1,455, probably an accurate body count according to newsmen who were at the scenes of many of the battles.

The four communist regiments are now reported regrouping on the Vietnamese side of the Cambodian border. No immediate threat of battle renewal is seen, but a new enemy offensive could be launched there in a few weeks, according to General Rosson.

That means that the three U.S. brigades now committed to Dak To will probably stay there, possibly one objective of the communists who are thought anxious to suck American troops out of the populated regions into remote corners. By this means, pacification work will slow down, as in the first corps region.

What else has the battle of Dak To meant?

If the enemy objective was indeed to overrun Dak To and eventually cut Vietnam in two parts, he has certainly failed in his mission. But if this was not his mission, if he had much more moderate aims, then he might have had more success.

The loss to the communists in Dak To was in manpower, a commodity they don't seem to be lacking. The Ho Chi Minh trail is believed clogged with infantry replacements.

There is no evidence that senior enemy officers were killed or captured in the fight, meaning that the four regiments might soon be ready to fight again.

Under these circumstances, the war of attrition that the Allied commander, General William C. Westmoreland, says he is fighting in Vietnam could prove disastrous in the view of many American officers who have been involved in the Dak To hill fighting.

One of the few surviving officers of the Second Battalion, 173rd Airborne Brigade, that fought on Hill 875, said that it would take two months to get his battalion back in fighting trim. Several other U.S. units were similarly hard hit.

Many American soldiers were outspokenly angry about having to fight in the tangled terrain of Dak To. "Why not bring in B-52s to knock this place down," one paratrooper asked as he fought his way up Hill 882.

Asked why he was carrying the fight into Dak To, General Peers commented to newsmen, "Why give the enemy another 15 miles of sanctuary?"

Senior Americans believe Dak To is another harbinger of the fights to come. The DMZ was the first, Dak To the second. Already enemy units are reported digging in in the hills of Quang Duc province due north of Saigon.

This could become another region for costly "submarine war."

Endit Arnett

sai

~~[struck through text]~~

(editors note: associated press photographer oliver noonan died while
covering a u. s. infantry company in the first day of a battle in the
foothills of central vietnam. ap newsmen horst faas and peter arnett
later covered the same action while looking for noonan's body. here is
their report of what happened to the outfit that noonan was with.)

breaking point

by horst faas and peter arnett

song chang valley, vietnam, aug. 24 (ap) -- all men have a breaking
point and nearly all soldiers of "a" company broke sunday morning.

"i am sorry sir, but my ~~men~~ refuse to go -- we cannot move out,"
reported lt. eugene shurtz jr. to the battalion commander over a crackling
field telephone.

                                                    51ST INFANTRY
at dawn, a company of the battle-worn third battalion of the 196th
light infantry brigade had been ordered to move once more down the jungled,
rocky slopes of nui lon mountain into a deadly labyrinth of north vietnamese
bunkers and trench lines. for five days in a row they had obeyed

BREAKING POINT

Peter Arnett and Horst Faas, "Breaking Point,"
Aug. 24, 1969. Typescript copy, Saigon Bureau Records,
Box 52, Folder 912. AP Corporate Archives, New York.

(Editor's note: Associated Press photographer Oliver Noonan died while covering a U.S. infantry company in the first day of a battle in the foothills of central Vietnam. AP newsmen Horst Faas and Peter Arnett later covered the same action while looking for Noonan's body. Here is their report of what happened to the outfit that Noonan was with.)

by Horst Faas and Peter Arnett

Song Chang Valley, Vietnam, Aug. 24 [1969] *(AP)* – All men have a breaking point and nearly all soldiers of "A" Company broke Sunday morning.

"I am sorry sir, but my men refuse to go—we cannot move out," reported Lt. Eugene Shurtz Jr. to the battalion commander over a crackling field telephone.

At dawn, A Company of the battle-worn Third Battalion 21st Infantry of the 196th Light Infantry Brigade had been ordered to move once more down the jungled, rocky slopes of Nui Lon Mountain into a deadly labyrinth of North Vietnamese bunkers and trench lines. For five days in a row they had obeyed orders to make this same push. Each time they had been thrown back by invisible communist soldiers who had waited through the rain of bombs and artillery shells for the Americans to come close to die in accurate crossfire.

In each assault Americans of A Company died, many attempting to drag wounded from under the enemy guns. Some still lay where they had died in front of the enemy positions.

Now it was Sunday, the sixth day of their battle. They wound (*sic*) not go back down the hill.

The battalion commander, Lt. Col. Robert C. Bacon, had been waiting impatiently for A Company to move out. Bacon had taken over the battalion only three days earlier after the former commander was killed. The battalion was still trying to reach the wreckage of the helicopter in which his predecessor, Lt. Col. Eli P. Howard, 41, of Woodbridge, Va., Associated Press photographer Oliver Noonan, 29, of Norwell, Mass., and six other men had perished.

This Sunday morning Col. Bacon was personally leading three of his companies to the helicopter wreckage.

He paled as the lieutenant's voice matter-of-factly told him that the soldiers of A Company would not follow his orders.

"Repeat that please," the colonel asked without raising his voice. "Have you told them what it means to disobey orders under fire?"

The lieutenant's voice from the bomb-scarred hill came back, "I think they understand—but some of them simply had enough—they are broken. There are boys here who have only 90 days left in Vietnam—they want to go home in one piece. The situation is psychic here."

The colonel asked, "Are you talking about enlisted men or are the NCO's (platoon and squad leaders) also involved?"

The lieutenant replied, "That's the difficulty here—we've got a leadership problem—most of our squad and platoon leaders have been killed or wounded in the past days."

A Company at one point in the fight was down to 60 men—half of its assigned combat strength.

Faced with the alarming situation, the colonel had recourse to severe measures—but instead he said quietly, "go talk to them again and tell them that to the best of our knowledge the bunkers are now empty—the enemy has withdrawn. The mission of A Company today is to recover their dead. They have no reason to be afraid. Please take a hand count of how many really do not want to go."

The lieutenant came back a few minutes later, "They won't go, Colonel, and I did not ask for the hand count because I am afraid that they all stick together even though some might prefer to go."

The colonel then said, "Leave these men on the

hill and take your [illegible] element (command post) and move to the objective."

The lieutenant said he was preparing to move and asked, "What do we do with the ammunition supplies? Shall we destroy them?"

"Leave it with them," the colonel ordered.

Then Colonel Bacon told his executive officer, Maj. Richard Waite, and one of his seasoned Vietnam veterans, SFC Okey Blakenship of Panther, West Virginia, to fly from the battalion base "LZ Center" across the valley to talk with the reluctant troopers of A Company. "Give them a pep talk and a kick in the butt."

This was the first time the men of A Company faced a field grade officer since the death of their former battalion commander on the first day of the battle.

They stood tired, bearded and exhausted in the tall blackened elephant grass. Their uniforms were ripped and caked with dirt.

"One of them was crying," said Sgt. Blakenship.

Then the soldiers told the two emissaries why they would not move.

"It poured out of them," the sergeant said. They told how they were sick of the endless battling in torrid heat, the constant danger of sudden firefights by day and the mortaring and the enemy probing at night. They said they had not enough sleep and that they were being pushed too hard, they hadn't had mail, they hadn't had hot food, the little things that had made the war bearable for them.

Helicopters brought in the basic needs of ammunition, food and water at a tremendous risk because of effective enemy ground fire. This was not enough for these men—they sensed that they were in terrible danger of annihilation and would go no further.

Maj. Waite and Sgt. Blakenship heard them out, looking at the men of A Company, most of them a generation apart, draftees 19 and 20 years of age with fear in their eyes.

Blakenship, a quick-tempered man, began arguing with the soldiers.

"One of them yelled to me that his company had suffered too much and that it should not have to go on," Blakenship recalled. "I answered him that another company was down to 15 men still on the move—and I lied to him—and he asked me, 'why did they do it?'"

The sergeant said he answered, "Maybe they have got something a little more than what you have got."

"Don't call us cowards, we are not cowards," the soldier howled, running toward Blakenship with his fists raised.

Blakenship turned his back and walked down the bomb-scarred ridge line to where the company commander waited.

The sergeant looked back and saw that the men of A Company were stirring. They picked up their rifles, fell into a loose formation and they followed him down the cratered slope.

A Company went back to the war.

End it/Faas/Arnett.

AP

WE'RE
TAKING FIRE

A Reporter's View of the Vietnam War,
Tet and the Fall of LBJ

PETER ARNETT
Author of **"SAIGON HAS FALLEN"**

Made in the USA
Monee, IL
28 February 2022